Praise for *P*

"I met Kemi over a decade ago and wa
presence and her ideas on what it take
Kemi has always epitomized grace and calmness—a quiet strength and assuredness that you can't help but feel more centered around. *POWER* is a reflection of this strength and assuredness, and it's my hope that we can all learn from this incredible guide and live and lead just a little bit more like Kemi!"

—Emma Isaacs, founder of Business Chicks

"Compelling, probing, and necessary. Kemi Nekvapil empowers us to step proudly from a life of doubt and learned smallness and into a life where we can unapologetically recognize and own our worth, courage, and the gift of our fullness."

—Madeleine Dore, creator of Extraordinary Routines

"This is a book about finding the power within you, no matter who you are or what may have happened to you. In an act of generous grace, Kemi Nevkapil demonstrates this process by sharing the way in which she tapped the great river of power that is her own soul. In *Power*, Kemi somehow manages to be blunt but gentle, galvanizing but calm, serious but hilarious, vulnerable but immensely strong. Reading this book will pull you into the flow of power we all share, to find the source that springs uniquely from your own life."

—Martha Beck, author of the *New York Times* bestselling *The Way of Integrity*

"Kemi shows us how we can claim our true power and agency without losing our hearts. *Power* is a beautiful call to action to live a more purpose-filled life."

—Marie Forleo, author of the #1 *New York Times* bestselling *Everything is Figureoutable*

"A practical guide on how we can reclaim power as individuals and harness more power as a collective. It's essential reading for any woman who wants to create change for herself and change for the world. You'll return to it for years to come."

—Susan David, psychologist at Harvard Medical School and author of the #1 *Wall Street Journal* bestselling *Emotional Agility*

"When I first met Kemi Nekvapil, I was captivated by her full aliveness, her warm humor, and her *power.* Not the kind of power we normally associate with the word; not a competitive, exclusive, dominating kind of power. Kemi radiates and teaches a different kind of power—she is a confident and courageous leader, and at the same time, she empowers, uplifts, and liberates others. This is the kind of power that will save our world and the kind she explores in her book. She teaches all of us how to honor our own values and voices, create boundaries and ask for what we need, and put our power in service of a world of inclusion and well-being for everyone."

—Elizabeth Lesser, cofounder of Omega Institute and author of *Broken Open* and *Cassandra Speaks*

"When I first met Kemi, I knew I was in the presence of someone more than special. She's a woman full of wisdom, grace, and good power. *Power* shows how you can become unstoppable by reclaiming your own power and living an authentic life."

—Jean Oelwang, founding CEO of Virgin Unite and cofounder of Plus Wonder

"This is an exceptionally POWERFUL book! Kemi is a powerful and unapologetic representation of what it means to be a FIERCE representative of LOVE. In this book, she creates a space for you to be the same through powerful storytelling, challenging your long-held beliefs and creating a safe space for self-reflection. This book is a divine gift to the world." —Koya Webb, author of *Let Your Fears Make You Fierce*

"I've seen firsthand the effect Kemi's work has had on so many women in my world. There is a reason Kemi is so adored—she challenges women to think about what's possible for their lives and then coaches them through the steps to get there. Powerful stuff (pun intended!)." —Sally Hepworth, author of *The Soulmate*

© PRUE AJA STEEDMAN

PENGUIN BOOKS

POWER

Kemi Nekvapil is a leading credentialed coach for female executives and entrepreneurs, a bestselling author, and a highly sought-after speaker. She has studied leadership and purpose at the Gross National Happiness Centre in Bhutan as well as with Dr. Brené Brown to become a Certified Dare to Lead™ Facilitator, working with teams and organizations to create daring leaders and courageous cultures. Kemi is a facilitator for The Hunger Project Australia and a regular interviewer of industry icons, including Elizabeth Gilbert, Elizabeth Lesser, Martha Beck, and Marie Forleo, and has worked with worldwide organizations including lululemon, Atlassian, Zoom, Dermalogica, and Omega. She is the host of the Audible Original podcast *POWER Talks*. With a level of compassion and wisdom gained only through extraordinary life experience and a twenty-eight-year yoga and meditation practice, Kemi is a powerful advocate for connected, value-based living.

POWER

A Woman's Guide to Living and Leading Without Apology

KEMI NEKVAPIL

FOREWORD BY ELIZABETH GILBERT

life

PENGUIN BOOKS
An imprint of Penguin Random House LLC
penguinrandomhouse.com

First published in Australia by Penguin Life Australia,
an imprint of Penguin Random House Australia, 2022
This edition with a new foreword by Elizabeth Gilbert
published in Penguin Books 2023

A Penguin Life Book

LIBRARY OF CONGRESS CATALOGING-IN-PUBLICATION DATA
Names: Nekvapil, Kemi, author.
Title: Power : a woman's guide to living and leading without apology / Kemi Nekvapil.
Description: [New York] : Penguin Books, 2023. | "First published in Australia by Penguin Life Australia, an imprint of Penguin Random House Australia, 2022"—Title page verso.
Identifiers: LCCN 2023021519 (print) | LCCN 2023021520 (ebook) |
ISBN 9780143138020 (paperback) | ISBN 9780593512111 (ebook)
Subjects: LCSH: Leadership in women. | Power (Philosophy) |
Self-actualization (Psychology) in women.
Classification: LCC BF637.L4 N44 2023 (print) | LCC BF637.L4 (ebook) |
DDC 303.3/4082—dc23/eng/20230602
LC record available at https://lccn.loc.gov/2023021519
LC ebook record available at https://lccn.loc.gov/2023021520

Printed in the United States of America
1st Printing

Set in Georgia Pro Light

This book is dedicated to:

any woman who has ever felt powerless, overlooked, unworthy . . .
any woman who is yet to step into her full power . . .
any woman seeking to make a greater impact . . .
any woman seeking to lead . . .
any woman striving for an empowered life.

For women of every race, color, age, creed, orientation, identification, and ability . . . this book is for you.

This book is for us.

Contents

Foreword

I met Kemi Nekvapil shortly before COVID-19 swept across the world and changed all of our lives forever. I was traveling through Australia on a speaking tour, and I was delighted to find out that she would be interviewing me onstage. At the time, I knew Kemi only through her on-paper résumé. I'd been told that she was a coach, a highly sought-after public speaker, an actor, a gardener, and a singer—all wonderful things, in my estimation. But when I encountered Kemi in person, I instantly knew that this was somebody far more special than any title (or string of titles) could ever convey. I was immediately captivated by this strong and beautiful woman, who emanated kindness, intelligence, grace, wit, and—yes—power. I'm sorry to report that everyone else in the room fell away as we tumbled into a delightful sense of intimacy—bonding over our shared love of high-end journals, exquisite pens, giddy humor, women's liberation, and the joys of wild travel. I knew she would be a friend from that moment on—and she has been. And I will never forget something Kemi said, right before we were about to go onstage together. She said, "I learned early on that I was never going to belong in any room I walked into because I was not like anyone else. And so I was just going to have to become myself."

Indeed, Kemi Nekvapil is not like anyone else. Born in England to Nigerian parents who dreamed of a better life for their children, she was raised by a series of White foster families who were sometimes kind and well-meaning, sometimes terrifying and threatening ("I could send you back to Nigeria"), but who always, always held all the power. She learned from earliest childhood that she must never upset the White people, while at the same time learning that no matter how perfectly she comported herself, she would never be fully accepted by that dominant, all-controlling culture. Nor, however, would she ever be fully accepted by her Black British neighbors, for she spoke and acted "too White," and her background was markedly different from theirs. Too African to be British, too British to be African (and that was before she confused matters further by moving to Australia!), Kemi spent her youthful years as a cultural nomad—constantly searching for belonging through compliance and people-pleasing—until the day she finally stopped trying to win the approval of a world that could never understand her and decided, instead, to lay claim to her own unique power.

In these pages, Kemi tells the story of how she learned over time to transform her differences into advantages, her "otherness" into empathy, her trauma into activism, her fear into courage, and her nearly impossible status as an outsider into the unflinchingly center-stage leadership role that she inhabits today. Forging a path where there was no path, she now generously extends a hand to women of all backgrounds who are coming up behind her. She is a keen and tireless guide to those who are feeling lost, overwhelmed, exiled, or misunderstood—in addition to being an inspiration to anyone who is ready for a complete revolution of consciousness, or a fierce self-awakening.

Kemi breaks down the five essential elements of POWER as Presence, Ownership, Wisdom, Equality, and Responsibility. I can personally attest that she does not merely admire these attributes, but fully embodies them. As a tireless student of life, she has met every challenge with a stubborn insistence to find the lesson in it—and then to pass that lesson along. A deeply spiritual soul, she has found her way through considerable difficulties by listening to a profoundly intimate interior voice. Generously, she shares that voice in these pages—offering hope in the form of a hard-earned, reality-burnished, gentlehearted wisdom that is touched by both laughter and tears.

It could not have been easy to write this book, or to bring it forth into print. It is not only Kemi's candor and vulnerability that are impressive to me; there are also the external pressures to consider. We live, unfortunately, in a world that will do almost anything to prevent women from having a voice. We also live in a world in which women of color who speak the truth will invariably be called "intimidating" or "angry" (as if there is nothing to be angry about). Indeed, Kemi reveals in this book that she has often been labeled "intimidating" simply by walking into a room. Before she even opens her mouth, many White people have decided that she is threatening: that's how severely her presence at the table makes the status quo tremble in fear. Given the violence and insidiousness with which White supremacy defends itself, it was no small act of courage for her to have written a book that is proudly and simply called *Power*. The title itself is an act of unblinking defiance, but it's also a beacon of light and love that will, I hope, draw others near, and will inspire ever more transformation and evolution within us all.

Truly, I believe that this book is a miraculous event—a divine gift, an act of creative generosity, and a rare treasure. Read it with an open mind and a brave heart, and watch your limitations fall away before your eyes.

Thank you, Kemi, for your beautiful work in the world. You are extraordinary, and I love you dearly.

Elizabeth Gilbert

Prologue

THE POWER OF THE MOTHER

I had felt the pull since I heard about this place. Being here, I knew I would be offered a new way of seeing the world and living in the world. I had come to the town with my family and our hosts, Ron and Beth, but I walked the half-mile-long path to this special place ahead of them. I knew I had to arrive there alone. I needed to arrive at this place without small talk—to see it for the first time in all of its glory, alone.

The atmosphere was typical of South India in January, heady with the scent of spices, jasmine, and frangipani. The path I took was edged with beautiful tropical trees and flowers. As I walked, I saw plants that I knew and loved, plants I knew and didn't love, and others I didn't know at all.

"I will never know all the plants," I lamented to myself.

Despite the beauty of the surroundings and the balmy Indian air, I found myself becoming impatient. I just wanted to get there. I knew the final destination was going to be a grand gift, and although I had no idea what that gift would be, I knew it would be a gift uniquely for me.

But where was it? Why was it taking so long to appear? I was getting tense and irritable, like a small child the night before Christmas. I then took a moment to "watch" myself, something I do often, and I laughed. There I was, anticipating so much the gift at the end of the path that I was feeling frustrated, because I was still on the path and the gift had not appeared yet. Then I caught a glimmer through a hedge, realized how close I actually was, and bowed my head. Now, I felt shy. I didn't feel ready.

Maybe I would be disappointed. Maybe I was wrong and there was nothing here for me at all.

And then I saw the whole structure, through a clearing in the trees, in all of its golden glory. My heartbeat quickened, and at the same time my breathing slowed. I was no longer feeling irritable. I was calm and I was ready.

The Matrimandir.

The Matrimandir ("Temple of the Mother") is an iconic nonreligious edifice in South India. It is a huge geodesic dome covered in golden discs, with every disc also covered with golden mosaic tiles a few inches wide. The golden dome is then surrounded by twelve petal-shaped meditation rooms.

Inside the central dome is the Inner Chamber, a meditation hall that contains the largest optically perfect glass crystal globe in the world. This unearthly structure, which symbolizes the birth of a new consciousness, was the vision of The Mother, previously known as Mirra Alfassa, who was born in a Jewish Egyptian-Turkish family in Paris in 1878. As an adult she moved to India, where the spiritual teacher Sri Aurobindo became her mentor. Sri Aurobindo saw her as his spiritual equal, named her "The Mother," and handed over all operations of his blossoming ashram to her. The Mother then founded the utopian township of Auroville in Puducherry (then called Pondicherry), where the Matrimandir stands.

The Matrimandir is a sight to behold. I give you full permission to put this book down and google it—it has to be seen.

Sometimes you know when you are about to be given the gift of an insight, a realization that will inform the next chapter of your life. On this day, I knew mine was coming. I didn't know what the message would be, but I was full of expectation.

When I arrived at the formal viewing spot, there were around twenty other visitors already there. But I wanted to be alone. I spied a solo seat carved from a single rock set away from everyone else that had my name on it. I walked slowly over to it; there was no need to rush now. I sat down on the rock seat without looking at the golden dome. I wanted to prepare myself, so I closed my eyes, breathed deeply several times, and took myself through a short meditation. As I inhaled and exhaled deeply, I said to myself, "Let me be open to what may reveal itself to me. Let it count."

And then, slowly, I opened my eyes.

As I gazed upon this incredible golden structure surrounded by its green lawns, I felt a sense of joy, peace, and possibility.

The joy I felt was for beauty. The peace I felt was for myself. The possibility I felt was for women.

The idea for the Matrimandir had been conceived by The Mother through visions. She saw it in her meditations; she did not "design" it. The Matrimandir was to be the symbol of the universal mother. It took thirty-seven years to build and she was ninety-three when the first stone was laid. The Matrimandir is built on four pillars, each with a meaning, and it is the meaning of the North Pillar that speaks to me most: "Her power of splendid strength and irresistible passion, her warrior mood, her overwhelming will, her impetuous swiftness and world-shaking force."

The Mother lived into her power by owning her leadership, by using her gifts of vision, communication, and hope. And in doing so she gave me and every woman the invitation to do the same: to birth our visions and communicate them in a way that empowers others to step into their power. She gave birth to a new consciousness, a new way to experience and show up in the world. My intention is that this book does the same for you—that it ignites in you a new way to experience and show up in the world.

The Mother had brought her vision—the Matrimandir—to life. Looking at it from that stone seat gave me everything I needed to carry out my vision. This book is my vision. Later, when we returned to our friends' home, I jumped onto the bed, grabbed my journal and pen, and began writing.

This is a book about power. This is a book about why we give it away. But it is also a book about why we need to own it, and how we ignite that power within others.

POWER

Introduction

ABOUT POWER

"The most common way people give up their power is by thinking they don't have any."

—Alice Walker

Women today have more opportunities than our mothers and grandmothers ever had, and yet the societal structures we must navigate to claim and own some of these opportunities can still lead us to question our abilities and our power. For many women, "power" is abstract. Many of us have been and continue to be intimidated by it. Throughout this book you will find that I have not used concepts of "soft power" or "personal power." This is deliberate. Power is power. We do not need to "feminize" it to make it more palatable; we need to redefine it. I want us to reacquaint ourselves with this word in a positive way.

Countless women were raised like me to believe that power belongs to others, that it is destructive, and therefore they had no interest in exploring or owning power for themselves. My relationship to power has mainly been one of *powerlessness*.

In my experience, power was White—either a White man in a suit, or a White woman who was blonde and thin. A college education also meant power—if you had a degree, you had more power than someone who didn't. Being able to get a college education was linked to privilege, which was linked to Whiteness, which in turn was linked to power.

At school I was Black, female, and overweight, and a college degree was not an option for me. Power, as it appeared to me then, was not a concept I recognized for myself. Over time I have needed to explore and define power on my own terms.

Julie Diamond is a woman whose work I admire when it comes to the subject of power—she is a leadership coach who has spent more than thirty years working in the world of human and organizational change. She is also the author of *Power: A User's Guide,* in which she writes: "Power is neither good nor bad; it is energy, a human drive to shape the world, influence others, and make an impact. We need power. Power may be difficult to master, but it's vital to have. It's generative and creative."

I like her explanation of power; it's so much more inclusive than what I had experienced or been led to believe. Add to that the *Oxford English Dictionary* definition of power—"the ability or capacity to do something or act in a particular way"—and we have something positive to work with. We all have the ability to do something or act in a particular way. So power is for all of us; it is not for the select few.

In my book *The Gift of Asking,* I talk about the struggle many women have with asking for what they need and want. One of the reasons for this struggle is the belief that to ask is to rock the boat, to no longer be seen as a "good girl." Being "good"—not asking for more, pleasing others, doing what we are told, and looking "good"—is a way for women to hold ourselves and each other powerless.

I have coached hundreds of women in my one-on-one practice and thousands of women in group settings. These are women in CEO roles, women running their own companies, entrepreneurs, managers, women on the land, professional athletes, yoga teachers, activists, social workers, and coaches—women in various positions in diverse industries. Rarely do these women start working with me to explore their power, but in the coaching process most uncover their relationship with power in the same way they uncover their relationship to asking. They explore the times they owned their power, when they had their power taken away, when they gave it away, how they have stepped into their power, and how life changes when they own and harness that power.

I am writing this book now at a place in my life where I am no longer going to pretend I don't have any power. And I am definitely no longer interested in being a good girl. And my intention is that by the end of this book, you'll step out of your version of being a "good girl" and step into becoming a fully expressed woman.

Power that is created by a system based on a person's gender, privilege, and "granted" status makes us believe it only belongs to a chosen few. And the continuity of this system depends on the chosen few inviting others who look like them and have the same upbringing as them to the power table. The rest of us are excluded. If you are reading this book, you are undoubtedly one of "the rest of us" and you know how the system works. You know how it affects us every day—the world we live in has been set up to keep us small. For many years I heard "The system is broken," but this is a rose-colored way of looking at things. It gives the impression that there was once, in the "days of old," a system that served everyone equally, and somehow one day, or even over a period of time, that system collapsed. But let's take off the rose-colored glasses and confront the truth. The system was meant to be this way; nothing got broken. The system was set up for men, it was set up for Whiteness. And the tragedy is that within that system, many of us have felt broken.

Whether you are reading this as a woman, a woman of color, a queer woman, a nonbinary person, or a disabled woman, you know. We all know what it feels like to be told we are broken. We internalize these myths—and when we do, we are complicit in the system and we keep ourselves exactly where we are told we belong.

I have learned, as many women have, how to live and lead "as an apology." Let me clarify what I mean here:

- I learned how to make myself small by not sharing my opinions, for fear of not being liked, because we are led to believe that being liked is our most important value.

- I learned to pretend I didn't have needs and wants because I didn't want to be told I was needy or difficult.

- I learned how to be a "good girl," to only do what was expected of me and toe the line.

- I learned how to apologize when speaking, diminishing the power of my words by smiling, or giggling "to soften my meaning" or my voice, or by actually apologizing before I spoke: "I'm sorry to say this, but . . ."

- I learned how to deny my leadership capabilities because my mind was fraught with the possibility of judgment and failure.

- I learned how to live "as an apology" as a Black woman navigating predominantly White spaces.

This was my version of living and leading as an apology. What does your version look like?

In contrast, what does living and leading *without* apology look like?

- It means that we take up space, without apology.

- It means that we communicate our needs because we are worthy of having our needs met.
- It means we operate in the world as full expressions of ourselves, creating our own unique paths.
- It means we own our opinions and voices, without diminishment or apology.
- It means that if we want leadership, we can step into leadership knowing that judgment and failure are part of the deal.
- It means that if we are called to leadership, we don't assume we are not good enough. We understand we will learn as we go.
- It means that we stand proud in our racial identity and ethnicity, and support others to do the same.

Now is the time to elevate our individual power and the power of other women, because the world needs women to own their power like never before. It is time we own our ability to "do something or act in a particular way," to build a better system from the inside out.

The shift from external to internal

I wrote this book to show you how I shifted the Power Stories I had about myself, so you can do the same with your own Power Stories.

Let's start by thinking about "external" power.

In 2019, I trained with Dr. Brené Brown to be a facilitator of her Dare to Lead™ leadership program. Brené Brown is a research professor and her work focuses on shame, vulnerability, and courage. She talks about the "power over" model, where people use shame and fear to wield *power over* others. We can see the results of this form of power everywhere, across the world, and the results of the fear of losing that perceived power. This is a power that sits outside of oneself. It can be taken away at any moment, which is why the wielders of this form of power hold on to it so tightly. Their perception of their own power is so fragile they need to use shame and fear to keep hold of it.

We don't need more of this kind of power in the world, and historically this form of power is created and perpetuated by men. Even back in the eighteenth century, the English writer, philosopher, and women's rights advocate Mary Wollstonecraft recognized this, declaring, "I do not wish women to have power over men; but power over themselves."

This form of power has led us to believe that there is only so much power to go around. In this system, if you have power, I can't have it, and vice versa. Many women who work or have worked within patriarchal structures have seen this form of power play out in every way. Some of these women were smart enough to know that they would need to play the "power game" to achieve their career ambitions. But to succeed, they had to perpetuate the idea that power was scarce and they "needed to protect their patch"—and perhaps as a result they were not able or willing to support other women in their careers. On top of that, the women "in power" would have felt isolated in a structure that was not built for women to thrive. There are many downsides to this type of power.

But power does not have to be an external force. When power is an *internal* force, it is an abundant resource: I can have it and you can have it too.

The power I want to guide you to cultivate through this book comes from building an internal force. A power built internally is stronger than any power bestowed from an external force.

Imagine a wall. Not fully formed.

To begin its life, a wall needs bricks, and bricks need to be made out of clay. Let's imagine that what forms the clay are your lived experiences, your ethnicity, your culture—everything that has made you who you are. But the clay needs to be formed into bricks: it is molded, like you have been, by your unique talents and accumulated skills over time. And what holds a wall together? Mortar. The mortar is your values—our values hold everything together.

Some of your wall will be built extremely quickly depending on your wall's location (where you were born in the birth lottery) and the help you receive from others (family, teachers, mentors). Other bricks will take decades to find their place. But they do have a place.

And your wall will be attacked: sometimes on purpose and sometimes by accident, sometimes by individuals and sometimes by a system or an environment that is out of your control. Your wall—your power—will feel damaged and broken until you remember that *you* formed the clay and the bricks and the mortar that built the wall in the first place, which means you can rebuild your power and reinforce your wall again and again and again.

Sometimes you will need support, as cracks start to show, or as the foundation is weakened. Sometimes you may need to make a new blend of mortar—redefine your values—at certain stages in life, but it's still your wall.

You are the builder of your power.

Writing this book

I have a deep relationship with words. I have an ear for words that are said and words that are unsaid.

It surely comes from being a professional coach for nearly a decade, but it also comes from growing up in a culture where only the "correct" and "proper" things were meant to be said. A culture where manners and niceties were respected more than the truth. A culture where I had to mind everything I said because of what was said about me and my "kind," because of what I was told about me and my "kind," and because of what I learned to believe about me and my "kind." I have a hearing for words unsaid because I am Black and English by birth.

When the title of this book came to me, I felt emotional, and nauseated. As soon as I'd thought of the word "power," my next thought was, "Who do you think you are to write a book about power?" And that was when I knew I needed to write it, because this is the book I was too scared to write.

When I sat down to unpack and write some of my stories for this book, I realized how often my powerlessness was to do with my race rather than my gender, though the two are very much connected. I have lived in this Black skin for nearly five decades and I have experienced many forms of racism. This includes having the N-word blatantly shouted at me from moving cars, all the way to the microaggressions (the daily, subtle slights I've experienced because of my race, which compound to cause harm) that are delivered with such subtlety I sometimes wonder if I am imagining them. It is possible for a person to gaslight themselves: to question their own reality if their lived experiences are routinely questioned by others.

As I began to write the stories of my life that involved the themes of power and race, a little voice within said, "If you write too much about being Black, it will make the White readers uncomfortable, and they won't like the book."

As a Black person, I have found it difficult to write about some of my lived experiences. I knew that if I was to write without fear, I had to tap into writers I admired. I am thankful to Maxine Beneba Clarke for writing *The Hate Race*, a memoir of growing up as a Black Afro-Caribbean woman in Australia in the 1980s. And as I embarked on writing this book I knew it was time to read *Why I'm No Longer Talking to White People About Race*, because I had a feeling author Reni Eddo-Lodge had put into words what I have struggled to say and write in the past. I participated in online writing courses with Roxane Gay and Ashley C. Ford to help own my life and my voice. These are two well-known and highly respected authors, both Black women, who write about their lived experiences without apology.

Apart from the broader experience of being a Black woman in a Western country, also know that "not wanting to upset the White people" comes from my childhood as a Black girl fostered to five different White families for my first eighteen years of life.

I was born in England to middle-class Nigerian parents in the 1970s. I was one of the tens of thousands of Nigerian children who were fostered in England. Nigerian parents fostered their children to White families through a network of "unofficial" caregiver families. My parents were like any others—they made decisions they thought would give their children the best opportunities in life. The ultimate plan for all of us children was that we would return to Nigeria and become its English-educated doctors and lawyers. I would see my birth mother during the school holidays when we would stay with her in her flat in London when she was in the United Kingdom. I have only one memory of spending time with my father—a great memory of a vacation in Paris, but only the one memory.

For the record, I have never resented my parents for the

decisions they made about my life. I have had other feelings, but never blame or resentment. I knew why they did what they did, and I know their choices came from a sense of parental duty and wanting to give the best to their children. Plus a healthy dose of the effects of colonization—a generation that was led to believe that British education was the best, no matter the sacrifice.

As a young child, my belief was that if I upset one White family, I would be moved on to another one, and another, and another. I was constantly threatened that I would be "sent back to Nigeria" by some of my foster parents, so I never felt secure or that I belonged anywhere.

For most of my life, I have felt the need to prove my right to be here—to be seen as an equal, to be accepted for who I am and not to be punished for who I am. And the fear of being punished for being Black is real. I had been writing this book for six months when George Floyd was murdered and Breonna Taylor was shot in her home while sleeping—two names in a list too long to comprehend, and here in Australia there are still too many police-related deaths of First Nations people. Being Black can be a crime in and of itself.

Fear of being punished for being Black is why I spent nearly two decades not wanting to be "too much." So I hid under the radar by "being good" so that I could "belong" without risk of being known.

Now that I am known to myself and others, I am always at risk. But for me, it is a risk worth taking to exist as myself. The risk is the gift.

So, for most of my childhood and formative years a voice was saying, "Do not upset the White people. If you do, you will not be loved." That voice is getting quieter as I get older and have learned to step into my power. And I will not allow that voice to write this book.

As an avid reader, I have found that the more an author shows of who they are—of their strengths and their weaknesses—the more permission the reader has to be strong and weak themselves. The more an author shares about their struggles in life, internally or externally, the more this allows me to reflect upon my own struggle. My intention is for you to examine how power has played out in your life through the lens of my life.

I am not an academic when it comes to the complexities of racism and how it debilitates individuals and whole races. I am not practiced at writing about race and power on a political or global scale, but I am the only one who can write this book within the context of my life, my experiences, my struggles, and my successes. And my intention, when I share and examine my stories about race, gender, and power, is to give you ownership of your race, gender, and power.

This is my life as I have lived it, and I am not going to apologize anymore.

May this book open doors for you to do the same—doors that lead you to places of validation, strength, affirmation, and possibility. But also, doors that open you up to the places where you have been afraid to go.

A message to my Black, Brown, and White sisters

If you are a woman of color reading this book and, like me, you live in a place of White majority, our journeys may have been different in the detail but our feelings and experiences will be similar.

I know you have been sidelined, overlooked, and patronized. I know you have been called "articulate" as if this wouldn't be expected. I know you have worked even harder than your White colleagues and been expected to prove your worth, only to then have your worth questioned. I know you have been the survivor of conscious and unconscious bias. I know you have internalized racism, and that this may have caused you to hate your appearance, question your talents, and want to hide your difference.

We survive racism and microaggressions nearly every day and the gaslighting is abundant and real. So this is a note just for you, in case you have forgotten.

You are worthy. You are smart. You are beautiful. And you are needed. Exactly as you are.

You and I must not hide anymore. We have gifts to bring.

This book is for you, and it's about all of us.

If you are a White woman reading this, you may already be on your journey of anti-racism, but if you're not, I invite you to learn how to empathize with the constant negotiations those of us who do not look like you have to make every single day. Our experiences are different from yours, and I invite you to get curious about that. Our lived experiences are not a threat to you. It is okay to be uncomfortable—we as women of color feel uncomfortable more often than you can imagine. I invite you to begin or continue your own journey, to learn about the systems that benefit you at the expense of others. Whether you are conscious of these systems or not, they exist.

I ask you to not interrogate your sisters of color. Please do not ask us to answer your every question about race relations, because we can't answer all of your questions. Sometimes we are still figuring it out for ourselves, and some of us have chosen not to answer these questions anymore, because the answering and justifying can render us powerless.

You can be a true ally for your sisters of color when you choose to see us fully—including the aspects of our lived experiences that make you uncomfortable—and we can all stand in our power together.

This book is for you, and it's about all of us.

No matter who you are, your age, your culture, ethnicity, sexuality, gender identity, or physical ability, your experience of power will shift as you read this book. If you are willing to go deeper, confront and own your lived experiences, honor the experiences of others, and be honest with yourself, you will emerge with a greater sense of your place and your power in the world.

How this book works

Power in its fullest, most complete form might appear intimidating, complex, or even unachievable, but breaking the concept of power down is the key to understanding how to build it. Building power is a layered process, so it's a matter of working on the bricks one at a time to build the structure. Power built from within can be broken into five primary Power Principles that together form the acronym of POWER:

Presence
Ownership
Wisdom
Equality
Responsibility

Each Power Principle is comprised of a number of focused components, and working on each of these builds the power within.

While recounting and compiling the stories around power from my own lived experience for this book, I realized that there are themes running through the stories. The acronym of POWER gave me the structure I needed to share the Power Principles in a way that can be implemented no matter where you are in your power story. Each principle is interconnected—when we are present, we take ownership; when we take ownership, we can trust our wisdom; when we trust our wisdom, we know we are equal; and when we know we are equal, we take responsibility for the transformation inside us, and the transformation we want and need outside of us.

Storytelling informs a large part of this book. Throughout history we humans have been guided by stories and the lessons they teach us. We learn through stories—they meet us exactly where we are and we hear what we need to hear from them, no more, no less.

Storytelling connects us to ourselves, each other, and the situations we find ourselves in. Along with my own Power Stories, I have invited past and present coaching clients to share their experiences of understanding and building their power during our work together. The stories are from a group of women who are diverse in age, ethnicity, career level, and industry. Each client has generously written down their own stories and given me permission to share them with you.

Throughout the book there are a series of Power Processes to follow to enrich your understanding and experience and set you on a path toward building your own power. Each process contains three questions and an invitation for you to take one action. Your answers to the Power Processes will lead you to the action. Your actions will lead you into your power.

You will notice throughout the book that I have put in dictionary definitions of certain words. Some of the stories I share are linked to what I believed certain words have meant, because of how they were used, or the assumptions I made about what they meant.

Clarifying the meaning of words has been a large part of my journey in understanding my experiences of powerlessness. I have found the practice of unpicking the meaning of words so freeing, and you may also find freedom in looking up the dictionary definitions of words that have rendered you powerless. As an English citizen, I was schooled in the Oxford Dictionary, to which I am very loyal. So although I know there are many other dictionaries of great renown, it is the *Oxford English Dictionary* for me. No apology.

As an author and a self-confessed (firstborn) rule follower, I want you to read the book from start to finish. I have crafted this structure to take you on a transformational journey, from one place to the next—one story, one question, one action at a time. But if you are a second-born rebel (or a rebel of any birth order), feel free to open the book at any section and trust that you will read exactly what you need in that moment.

When you have finished this book, hold on to it. Use it as a lifelong reference for when you are feeling diminished or powerless. Open a chapter that speaks to you. Ask yourself the questions in the Power Processes, and your answers will guide your next action. This is self-coaching—the ability to ask yourself the questions that cut through, take action on the answers, and lead yourself toward your power.

My promise

I know your time is precious, so I will let you know now: if you are hoping this book includes top tips to "slay the enemy," or tactics and strategies about an old form of power, it is not the book for you. This book is for you if you are willing to go deep inside and see who you have been, who you are, and who you are becoming.

It is not my job to tell you how to build your power. It is my job to create a space for you to do this for yourself through deep listening, exploring assumptions, challenging beliefs, sharing stories, asking questions, and creating space for reflection. As a coach, my role is to walk alongside women and remind them of who they are, what they want to achieve, and how they want to show up for themselves and others. I have the honor of working with strong, intelligent, driven, and kind women every day. But this doesn't mean that they are not sometimes afraid, confused, lost, and overwhelmed—I work with humans, not robots.

Sometimes coaching feels like magic. It's the connection and power that occurs when someone feels truly heard and someone else truly listens.

This is my promise to you:

> I promise you, if you are willing to do the work, this book will give you access to building and owning your power without apology.
>
> I promise you this book will give you permission to stand within yourself, with gravity, grace, and self-respect.
>
> I promise you this book will give you the ability to transform what you have seen and experienced as power in the past and the confidence to create something else—a power that is born within you, a self-generating force, a power you can be proud to own.
>
> I promise to guide you along the way.

Part 1

POWER PARADIGMS

"I do not wish women to have power over men; but power over themselves."

Mary Wollstonecraft

I.

MY FIRST LESSONS IN POWER

Nigger (noun—offensive): A contemptuous term for a Black or dark-skinned person. The word "nigger" has been used as a strongly negative term of contempt for a Black person since at least the eighteenth century. Today it remains one of the most racially offensive words in the language.

Darren Page was a short teenager of about fifteen years of age and had more power than I knew any other person of that age to have: he was White and he had a gang. When I say "gang," I don't mean in the contemporary American sense—there were no drugs, guns, or knives. The gang was just a group of four to five teenage boys. But as an eleven-year-old girl, they were a gang to me, with their persistent words their weapons of destruction.

Darren Page was never "Darren" to me. He was always "Darren Page"—I would never have dared to call him only by his first name. In fact, I never even used his name to his face. I knew my place.

We went to the same school, and lived near each other in a working-class suburb in the English county of Kent. The Grove, as we called it, was a circle of houses with a park in the middle. It was a park of the 1980s, which meant the play equipment was simple, fun, and dangerous. It definitely wouldn't meet today's safety standards. There were baby swings with a concrete slab underneath, larger swings with another concrete slab underneath, and a huge slide with a metal runway that burned your bum in summer and was too cold to use in winter. It also had a concrete slab at the end. The area doubled as Darren Page's headquarters.

I would often play in the park with my best friend Anne and her brother Alex. Anne and Alex lived on the other side of the park, so the park in the middle was our natural meeting place. We were good friends, if you ignored the constant power games that Anne played; she would change her mind at random intervals about whether I was her best friend or not. Thanks to living in foster families from an early age, I had a strong internal need to be "chosen," to belong, and to be chosen by Anne gave me the ultimate sense of belonging.

But being in the park, making up plays and songs, seemingly content in the world of our collective imaginations, also involved the ever-present threat of Darren Page. His house was on a hill that overlooked the park, so you could always see him coming, and the three of us were always on high alert for his arrival. I have various memories of what would happen when Darren Page approached us. On some occasions all three of us would run—as fast as we could—to one of our houses and take cover (which house we ran to depended on how much time we had to escape once we had seen him appear). We usually had between one and three minutes to make it, depending on the pace at which he and his gang moved.

But whether we had one or three minutes, I could always hear the racist insults ringing in my ears as my legs moved as fast as they could.

"Oh, the fucking nigger is here!" Darren Page would shout. "I thought I could smell something!"

"Is it the smell of monkeys?" another voice would yell, as they all laughed.

"Sticks and stones may break my bones, but names will never hurt me," the rhyme goes. But those words did hurt me—they were the soundtrack to my childhood. Growing up as "the only one in the village" takes its toll.

Other times, I would be determined to stay, defiant in my right to be in the park. I would be on the swings with Anne and Alex, as Darren Page and his gang approached.

"We are staying this time," we would say to each other. "We are staying."

Darren Page and his gang would form a circle around us, at which point we had no choice but to stay. What had felt like a determined power move on our part suddenly became our downfall. Now we had to stay and we couldn't go anywhere. We would continue to swing back and forth cautiously as they harassed, bullied, and belittled me with their racist comments and attacked Anne and Alex for being with me.

Occasionally we would do our best to talk back to them, but they were older and crueler. It was obvious to all of us, them and us, that we were completely powerless. They had the power.

We were never able to hold our resolve for long. Soon enough, one of us would be so affected by what was being said that we would leave, and the others would follow. Sometimes we left crying. Sometimes we screamed insults back, which they ridiculed. Sometimes we just walked off in silence, filled with a rage that had no words.

Being a Black foster child in 1980s England was nothing to envy.

I wonder now what Anne and Alex thought about all of this. They chose to be my friends, which was brave of them—they were White but were bullied by association.

But our friendship was confusing for me. I believed that Anne must be my real friend if she was willing to associate with me, and yet she was always playing power games with me. I would do anything for her approval, which is how I made my first early foray into shoplifting. At eleven years old, I was still very much in love with my baby doll (a White baby doll), but Anne made it very clear that I had to grow up and shoplifting was the way to grow up. I think my first "assignment" was to steal sweets. I succeeded. And I hated it.

When I was eventually caught shoplifting, it was for my loot of fruit-smelling stationery, popular in the 1980s. Loved stationery then and love stationery now. I was walking out of the store when the shopkeeper's hand landed on my shoulder. I can still feel the pressure of that hand today and remember the shame of that moment.

Shoplifting was never a "cool" thing for me. I did it because I wanted to belong to someone—Anne—and this was the price of admission. When waiting to be picked up by the police, all I kept thinking about was that my foster parents would send me and my sister away. At this time we were with a foster family who constantly threatened to send us "back to Nigeria," even though we had both been born in England. But as I traveled in the police car back to our foster family to face the music, the policeman gave me an even scarier outcome to mull over.

"I could separate you and your sister, and you will never see each other again," he said.

I did not want to be sent "back to Nigeria," a place that had been demonized for me by White people for my whole childhood, but I would go anywhere if it meant my sister and I would stay together. At the time I had no idea that the policeman didn't have the power to separate us. But I did know that he had more power than me, so I believed him.

One thing I do remember vividly of those times is that no adult ever stood up for me. No grown-up ever told Darren Page that what he was doing was unacceptable. No one made me feel that we were allowed to be in the park just as much as anyone else. It was 1980s England, I was Black, and that was just the way it was. I never told my foster parents about the racist abuse I faced on a daily basis at the park or at school. I believed that was the way it was, that as a "blackie" and a "golliwog," I would be tolerated at the best of times—nothing more. I did not want to be a burden to my foster parents, so much of a burden that they would pass us on to more strangers or "send us back to Nigeria."

It is said that when a person finds themselves near the bottom of a power structure (as I was), their need for dignity and survival induces them to find someone they think is even lower than they are.

By sheer luck, Ruth moved to our street.

Ruth's house was a little farther away than the rest of ours. She could see our house, Darren Page's house, and Anne and Alex's house from her front garden. Her house was not quite in the circle of houses around the park that made up The Grove, so location-wise she didn't quite belong. And when she moved in, it was decided that she and her family were "pikeys," an offensive slang term used for Gypsies. Ruth's family were not culturally Gypsies, a group with a rich and colorful history that experienced significant discrimination themselves throughout the 1980s. But they were called "Gypsies" because they were poorer than the rest of us. That made them the lowest of the low.

The first time I met Ruth, I remember how shy and pretty she was—any blonde girl was pretty in my eyes. But her clothes and face were dirty. It was obvious her family had less money than the rest of us.

Ruth never did anything to any of us. All she wanted was to be invited to play and to be accepted and to belong, just like me. But, sadly, that was never going to happen, because I sensed that she was even lower than me on The Grove hierarchy and I had a chance to exploit the minuscule opportunity for power that I had.

Acting friendly and innocent, we would call on Ruth and invite her to the park. The first few times she was openhearted, enthusiastic, and eager to play with her new neighbors. But as time went by, her enthusiasm waned because our idea of "play" was to treat her like an object of ridicule, not a friend.

We were horrible to her. We would taunt, bully, and shame her about everything we could: her clothes (even though most of mine were from charity stores before that was considered cool), her house (you could smell the "unwashed" smell from the street), her lisp, her parents. We picked her apart in every way we knew how, because it made us feel powerful. Now I had power, just like Darren Page.

Then one day I had this idea that was so good, so funny, it was going to be remembered forever. I told Anne and Alex about the plan and I was so proud. It was genius—the ultimate humiliation for Ruth and the ultimate power play for me.

When we all arrived at Ruth's house, she didn't really want to come out with us. But her mum encouraged her to "go and play with the nice children." We walked her to the side of the park near our house and offered her candy wrapped in shiny paper. She was hesitant, but we insisted. Eventually she agreed to eat it.

I remember my eyes darting between the candy, Ruth's face, and the faces of my accomplices as she started to unwrap it. I was praying that she couldn't see or smell what we had done. I couldn't smell it, so I assumed she couldn't either. She hesitated, as anyone would if they were surrounded by a group of notoriously mean "friends" and were being made to eat something no one else was eating.

She put the candy in her mouth and we were all silent.

Until one of us couldn't hold it in anymore: "You just ate dog shit!"

We all laughed at her. "You smell like shit and you eat shit!"

She spat out the candy.

I saw her face reddening. I heard our laughter and saw our pointing fingers.

Then I saw the tears form in her eyes and I watched as they fell.

And I stopped laughing.

Her eyes were locked with mine, pleading, "What have I ever done to you? Why would you do this to me?"

And my eyes replied, "I needed someone else to feel like shit for once."

Ruth ran home as the three of us celebrated our genius. But before long, I was thinking how it didn't feel as good as I thought it would. I had stepped into Darren Page's shoes for a few moments because I wanted to feel like him. I wanted to have that power. But as seductive as that idea was, in that moment I knew it just wasn't me. Gaining that kind of power meant giving up who I was.

I knew what I had done was bad. I had terrorized Ruth for no other reason than to elevate my status in The Grove, in my world. But it didn't feel comfortable. I felt like I was a bad person, and those feelings triggered many thoughts. Maybe I was fostered because I was bad? Maybe Darren Page always ran me out of the park because I was bad?

Maybe I was the piece of shit all along. I had just proven how bad and dirty I was. And Ruth had seen it too; she had told me with her eyes.

The thing is, control and command were the only forms of power I had ever been shown and I didn't know any better. But now that I had tasted that form of power—belittling others to feel better about myself—I realized it didn't make me more worthy and it didn't make me powerful. It made me feel like I was the lowest of the low, the absolute reverse of my intended outcome.

What I needed to learn was that there are other forms of power. I needed to know about the power that I could build within myself for the benefit of others, but that was a long time coming.

II.

THE POWER OF OPPRESSIVE STRUCTURES

> *"Patriarchy kills off stories and women to maintain its power. If you're a woman, this stuff shapes you; it scars you, it tells you that you are worthless, no one, voiceless, that this is not a world in which you are safe, equal or free."*
>
> **—Rebecca Solnit**

A part of me did not want to write about patriarchy in this book, but you can't write a book about women and power without writing about patriarchy.

Patriarchal systems are one of the most powerful ways women are kept in line. In them, we are given a very small box in which to express ourselves and operate in the world. How we look, how much we weigh, what jobs we can and can't do, what is "feminine" and what is "other" are all decided for us. And if we dare to create our own ways of being in the world, if we dare to self-express how we want, weigh as much as we want, say what we want, and work where we want at whatever level we want, the punishment is exacting and vengeful—and above all, predictable. It is the ultimate *power over* model and it does its job: it keeps many women quiet, in their place, and slowly rotting from the inside out.

But it isn't only the patriarchal model that does this to women. We also do it to ourselves and to each other through our internalized patriarchy.

Internalized patriarchy is not about naivete or a lack of intelligence. It doesn't matter where you are on the journey to gender equality, you will have your own form of internalized patriarchy.

As part of my research for this book I sent out a question via text message to family, friends, and close colleagues ranging in age from fifteen to fifty-three. Many of them are successful women who work in diverse industries, such as public service, law, music, education, creative arts, real estate, and business.

The question I asked was "How does your internalized patriarchy show up in the world?" I had hardly put my phone down after pressing "send" when the responses came flying in:

> "Don't worry about the big things/questions/actions. Men will take care of it. I was raised by strong patriarchs who meant well by it, but cut me off at the knees in the process."

> "Recently, I was told that as a woman, I should never show emotion at work because I wouldn't get promoted beyond my current role. To me, that internal voice is now saying, 'As a woman, you will never be taken seriously because men can do a better job than you.'"

> "For me it's that there's 'no space for me in a man's world.' That's what stopped me from becoming a photographer when I was eighteen."

> "I have to make them like me. Saying what I want to say will make them angry."

> "What is the point? They rule the world."

> "Don't ask for too much."

"Your feelings don't matter."

"I was once told, as a teenage girl, 'Whatever you do, don't grow up to be a woman.' I don't think I synthesized that as truth in an ultimately damaging way, but it certainly communicated to me that of all the terrible things I could grow up to be, growing up to be a woman was the worst."

"Male approval is essential."

"Men can do anything they want. This relates to my past and sadly recent experiences."

"Men offer protection."

"Men have the answers."

"Men determine my desirability."

"I have to be thin."

"Men validate me."

"I should be the property of a man."

"My identity as a woman is defined by a man."

"Men define what's worthy and valuable: to be worthy I have to be valued by men. Also, when in a leadership position at my college, I had the strong belief that I had to be utterly beyond reproach to be maybe good enough as a female leader. Men could be very flawed as leaders but still be good enough; I had to be perfect and even that might not be enough."

One of the responders wrote at the end of her response: "I have so many. It makes me so, so sad." I shed a tear or two as these responses came in. I picked up the phone to speak to a couple of the responders, and we shed a tear together, which led to mutual anger and laughter at how destructive and ridiculous it all was.

My internalized patriarchal narrative has included various forms of "Men know best." I know I'm not alone in this one.

When I think of these internalized experiences, they affirm to me how important it is that we each acknowledge how we have our own internalized misogynistic and patriarchal narratives. Owning our version is our foundational stone to building a power that transcends this debilitating form of *power over* women.

What is important is that we are fully aware of when and how we take power away from ourselves and other women when we believe in these oppressive systems.

And while we are on the delightful topic of patriarchy, this is a perfect segue into another type of *power over*—racism.

III.

THE POWER OF RACISM

Racism (noun): **1** Prejudice, discrimination, or antagonism by an individual, community, or institution against a person or people on the basis of their membership of a particular racial or ethnic group, typically one that is a minority or marginalized. **2** The belief that different races possess distinct characteristics, abilities, or qualities, especially so as to distinguish them as inferior or superior to one another.

I knew from a very young age that I was different, and not in a good way. Not in the way that children are now told "different is good." I was different in a bad way.

My internalized racism was formed from what White people kept telling me: that I was a Black one, but a good one. That was a narrative I wanted to step into. I wanted so badly to be good, so that I could somehow balance out what I could not change—the "badness" of being Black. I knew I was inferior—I had been told many times—but if I could overwhelm everyone with my goodness, maybe they wouldn't see my skin color. What if my goodness could trump everything else?

During the eruption of Black Lives Matter in 2020, I heard a Black psychologist say, "If you are Black in a White world, you may find that aspects of yourself that you thought were your personality are actually ways of managing the trauma of racism."

I remember stopping what I was doing as I processed this. I remember knowing he was right, that my "goodness" had not been a personality trait but a way of existing in a world where I was told repeatedly, in subtle and not-so-subtle ways, that I did not belong.

And in the same way that patriarchy can lead to internalized patriarchy, experiencing racism can lead to feelings of internalized racism. This is how mine showed up a few years ago. As a previously self-published author and a lover of writing letters, I had a great relationship with my local post-office owners CC, Rich, and Jake. They had helped me send off thousands of books and letters over many years, watching my children grow up as they frequented the post office with me.

One day I walked into the post office and an Asian man was with Jake behind the counter. Jake let me know that the post office had been sold, and this man and his wife would be taking over. They were currently in a handover period and Jake was showing them the ropes.

My first thought was, "I don't want things to change. I love coming here."

My next thought was, "As they are Asian, there'll be no relationship as 'they' keep to themselves and don't like Black people."

And there it was. My internalized racism. I was making the same narrow assumptions about Asian people (and yes, "I have Asian friends") that people make about me as a Black woman.

At dinner that night, I shared these thoughts with my family and, of course, they were unimpressed. But I didn't tell them to impress them. I told them so that they could understand that racism is not always aggressive or visually oppressive; it can manifest in your unfounded thoughts about the young couple who have just bought the local post office.

Voicing these thoughts to my family was powerful, because once I had said it out in the open, I knew it was not the way I wanted to be in the world. I decided that I was going to build a relationship with the new post-office owners, and I have. Tommy and Fay are great business owners and I enjoy talking to them as much as I did CC, Rich, and Jake.

Internalized racism is common among those of us who have experienced racism, and noticing this in yourself and others is the first step. Many years ago when I was visiting England, a fellow Nigerian went into a tirade about how "the Sudanese" were taking jobs.

I stopped dead in my tracks. Dumbfounded, I looked at her and said, "What? That is not even your voice! That's what White people say about Black people, and now the Black people are saying it about the Black people?"

Recognition of our internalized misogyny, patriarchy, and racism is more powerful than the denial of our internalized misogyny, patriarchy, and racism.

When we own up to the power of these destructive forces, we have the power to change them.

IV.

REDEFINING POWER

We need to redefine power. If we don't, we will constantly believe power belongs to the chosen few.

Power belongs to us all. We must not wait to be chosen by those who have *power over*: we must choose it ourselves. We don't need to be a certain age, race, gender, sexuality, or of a certain physical ability to enhance our power for ourselves and others.

No one who is invested in the old form of *power over* is going to grant you or me permission to use power. We need to give permission to ourselves—permission to redefine a structure that not only limits women, but also limits men.

If we are to redefine power, where do we begin? If it is no longer about having *power over* somebody, what can power become?

If we are to claim our right to power, we need to be willing to accept that these structures have diminished women and marginalized people in many ways. We have, to a point, consciously and unconsciously perpetuated these structures, either due to fear or due to comfort—an unwillingness to rock the boat and push beyond our comfort zone. There is something comfortable about "knowing your place," even if "your place" is restrictive and destructive to you.

My journey to power started on the inside. It had to, as so many systems exist to oppress me as a woman and as a woman of color. It has been essential for me to dismantle the power structures I have been born into, believed in, and, in some cases, perpetuated.

I have needed to unpick my relationship with power, my role in it and outside of it, before I could rally against that form of power and build something empowering. When I have gone within and done the work, my power has strengthened and grown.

The reality is that the old form of power will always be at work outside of us. We must always strive to do our own internal work, and yet the structures outside of us—the external—may still have their grip on us. That's why it is so important to surround yourself with women who are striving to build and master their power and own their place, while at the same time supporting you to do exactly the same, master *your* power. It is then that we will be able to dislodge external power structures.

The incident with Ruth when I was eleven years old taught me that *power over* does not feel good, but Darren Page's bullying taught me that being overpowered doesn't, either. This book redefines power and lays out a clear process that allows us to rethink it and build a structure that will guide, enable, and empower all of us.

I want us all to understand the truth of our power. I want us to own it for ourselves and use it well.

We want to build power-filled lives, not power-fueled lives.

We want to work within ourselves and use our power as a regenerative resource, instead of working externally to dominate, using power as a limited resource.

That is the difference between "doing" power and "being" power.

V.

THE POWER ACRONYM

Looking at power through the lens of the POWER acronym sets it apart from what we have been told—that power is "done to" people. It opens us up to how we as individuals and communities can shift the structure in a way that benefits and empowers more people.

The Power Principles that form the acronym show us how to build power from the inside out. We are practicing power, building power, and feeling power at various stages throughout the Power Processes. This is not a linear experience. You may experience quantum leaps into your power, but there will also be small steps forward and backward—in and out of power—throughout this process. This structure will be here to hold and guide you.

P is for PRESENCE

To be present is to be aware in the moment, to acknowledge what is at play internally and externally. Our presence (or lack thereof) dictates our ability to connect with ourselves and with others.

O is for OWNERSHIP

Ownership is the ability to integrate all parts of ourselves. As we explore our stories—those we have lived, those we are told, and those we have created—we take full ownership of who we have been and who we are becoming.

W is for WISDOM

We all have an inner wisdom that has the power to direct us through our lives. Too often we give that power away, but if we learn to trust ourselves, our innate wisdom will lead us.

E is for EQUALITY

We all have a role to play in shaping global equality, in seeking it for those who have less than we do. We also have a role to play in owning the equality that sits within each of us, no exceptions.

R is for RESPONSIBILITY

When we take full responsibility for our power, we have the freedom to decide how we use it. We all have the ability to do something or act in a particular way.

Power, as redefined here, sits with you and me. We can use this power as individuals and we can use it as a collective.

The patriarchy is purpose-built to support itself, not to support us. We are the ones responsible for dismantling it—with our presence, ownership, wisdom, equality, and responsibility.

When women become responsible for what needs to change, things change. We don't need anyone to save us: we can save ourselves and each other. I do not need you to be responsible for me, because that disempowers me. I want you to be responsible *with* me.

We can do the work. We have always been able to do the work.

VI.

TIME FOR A NEW PARADIGM

Paradigm (noun): A typical example or pattern of something; a pattern or model.

The best way to transform a paradigm is to start on the inside—awareness holds the key to all internal shifts. Being aware of why we do what we do is the first step to change.

To start with, I want us to question who we think deserves power, and then picture what a new paradigm of power could look like. It could be:

- Women believing in themselves and their agency.
- Women believing that they belong wherever they want to be.
- Women owning multiple forms of power.
- Women supporting, mentoring, and coaching each other into power.

We need to keep shaking things up. We can't settle for the status quo—it doesn't serve us and it doesn't serve men.

How do we do this?

We need to stand in all of the rooms we want to be in, celebrate our presence there, and invite more women to stand with us.

This is how we shift a paradigm.

One power-filled woman at a time.

Part 2

PRESENCE

"In the presence of your own loving attention, you create the inner conditions that are necessary to step into the next greatest evolution of yourself."

Debbie Ford

I.

P IS FOR PRESENCE

To be present is to be aware in the moment, to acknowledge what is at play internally and externally. Our presence (or lack thereof) dictates our ability to connect with ourselves and with others.

Presence is not the easiest aspect of power to grasp or define, because it is, in some ways, intangible. Presence is a way of being and feeling. It is a state of being exactly in the moment, without thought of the past or the future.

As a coach, I know that the presence I bring to a coaching session is what creates a safe space for my clients. My ability to be present is one of my most treasured disciplines—it gives me the ability to be one hundred percent there with the person I am speaking with, without judgment or agenda, allowing them to share their full humanity, so that they feel safe, heard, and seen.

In the book *Maybe You Should Talk to Someone*, the author, Lori Gottlieb, writes about being a therapist while also being in therapy herself. I fell completely in love with this book. One of the many moments that really affected me was when the author wrote, about her clients and people in general, that "in a state of perpetual distraction, they seemed to be losing the ability to be with others and losing the ability to be with themselves." It got me thinking that perhaps we have not always been in a "state of perpetual distraction." We used to take for granted the opportunities to be present; it was never something we had to put boundaries around or actively cultivate the way we do now. Our devices have replaced our ability to be present—the scrolling, swiping, and tapping allowing us to be continuously distracted from ourselves.

Who are you when you are present to yourself? Who are you when you are present to others?

Presence is not about meadows filled with flowers or a serene experience of blissed-out enlightenment. Being present can be confronting, uncomfortable, confusing, and challenging. That's why we relish these opportunities to be distracted from ourselves and others.

As women, our ability to be present to ourselves is trained out of us from an early age: we are socialized to be of service and present to the needs of others. Being of service is wonderful, but we must also learn to be present to who we are, what we need, what we want to give, and what we have to give. (The last two are not the same.)

When we are present to ourselves, we are aware of our thoughts, feelings, dreams, desires, pain, despair, grief, and internal chatter.

When we are present to others, they let us in on *their* thoughts, feelings, dreams, desires, pain, despair, grief, and internal chatter. Our presence allows others to feel respected and safe.

When we are present, we can ask ourselves questions: *How am I? Am I fearful? About what? Anxious? About what? What are my dreams? What do I want?* And another question we must ask ourselves is: *Who am I when I'm not present to myself and others? What am I missing?*

Cultivating presence is the first step to building power. The stories that follow demonstrate the impact of presence. None of the qualities and offerings I share in the following pages are fully available to us unless we are present. It is impossible to fully experience empathy, self-awareness, or delight, or access the power of the mirror or the pause without being present.

The Power Stories within this principle focus on the experiences of Meredith, Jessica, and Maddy. Each story highlights how the ability to be present—to our thoughts, to what is missing from our lives, and to learning how to pause—has made a transformational difference to each of them.

Presence is powerful. It informs our ability to stand in our power and with the power of others. It is worth practicing.

II.

THE PRACTICE OF PRESENCE

Developing presence takes commitment and effort; it is a constant practice. We are all different, and practicing presence or developing practices that encourage a sense of presence will take different forms for different people.

A few practices I have that help me to develop and practice presence are yoga, meditation, journaling, and gardening.

There are many practices of yoga, each with different physiological effects and different ways of steering the mind. Although I enjoy many forms of yoga, I find the most effective for building presence are the practices built on repetitive sequences—similar to sun salutations, where you know the exact movement that is coming next. When you know what movement is coming next, you don't have to think about it, which gives you the chance to be present to what is happening in your mind and body.

I have been practicing yoga and meditation for twenty-five years. Depending on my life stage, my yoga practice over the years has danced between a two-hour daily practice at 4 a.m. to just one daily sun salute. But how long we practice or where we practice is not as important as the practice itself; it is the compounding effects of yoga and meditation that make the difference. Presence is a superpower and yoga and meditation will feed that power.

Meditation can create a space for us to be in touch with our power in a mindful way. In the early days of my practice, I believed that meditation was only worthwhile if I committed to an hour a day, which meant I rarely did it. But similar to my yoga practice, my meditation practice has changed and evolved depending on my season of life. I have meditated for five minutes in the parking lot after dropping off young children to school, I have meditated for eight hours a day at a ten-day retreat (a little too much for me) and every length in between. At this stage in my life, my practice is seated meditation for twenty minutes, five days a week. I have never aspired to flowing orange robes and a mountaintop with my meditation practice. I have aspired to self-awareness—to be present to what I am thinking and feeling and to be aware of my relationship to myself and how I am going in life. For me the biggest gift of meditation is that it connects me to myself before I connect with others. It allows me to be of service to myself before I serve others. It fills me up, so I can give from a grounded and generous place of presence.

Another practice that has helped me bring focus on being present is journaling—a practice I have had since I was a child. Writing down my thoughts, feelings, aspirations, and moments of gratitude is very grounding and allows me to be present to my current reality. I rarely go back and read my journals—for me, that's not the point of journaling. What I gain is the practice of being present in the moment. For the last few years I have mainly journaled straight after my meditation, but I have done it before my meditation too. I have journaled in the middle of the day, before going to bed, at airports, in parks, at the theater. I always write by hand. Sometimes I subscribe to Julia Cameron's "three pages a day" structure from her book *The Artist's Way*; other times I focus on writing three moments of gratitude or affirmations for the day. It is not the "how" of journaling that brings presence, it's the act of journaling that does this.

We need to know where we want to make improvements, what is working in our lives and what isn't, because knowing this affects where we are heading. So many of us live life by default unless we are aware of what is driving us or what is burdening us. I have found that these methods of being present have helped me to confront, analyze, and take action in my own life.

For example, sometimes I ask myself questions before I sit down to meditate—perhaps a dilemma I have at the time. I don't meditate on the question, I sit in silence and breathe. But when I have finished meditating, I have the answer. In some ways I am not a naturally tolerant person, but learning to be still and patient has made me more tolerant, and I hope more tolerable to others!

When working with clients, I've noticed that asking them, "What are you tolerating?" often reveals interesting answers. This question creates space for the client to be present to how they feel about certain aspects of their lives and their circumstances.

One client I was working with told me it was the best question she had ever been asked, because her answer changed the trajectory of her life. She started journaling her answers to the question and realized that she was tolerating most of her life: her work, her relationship, and her health. These are fundamental life pillars for most of us. Once she was present to this, she was able to make the changes she wanted to make, including leaving her job, going into couples counseling with her partner, and booking an appointment with her doctor—all of which led to her taking charge of her life in the areas that meant the most to her.

Because of these practices, I can be present to the thoughts and feelings of others without judgment, as I have learned to be present to my own thoughts and feelings without judgment. This is what I have found incredibly powerful about yoga and meditation and journaling: the ability to be with myself and be with others.

My final practice for cultivating presence is tending my

garden, which I call my third child. When my husband and I were buying our current home, a deciding factor for me was the garden. The house had been owned by an Italian man who had created the garden with great love and care over fifty years. I felt excitement and an incredible responsibility to build on what he had created. For over twenty years, I have been deep into the rabbit hole of organic gardening and I hope to never come out. Being present in nature and being present to nature are two of the many benefits of gardening. When creating a partnership with nature, we are reminded that we are a part of something much bigger than ourselves. We are a part of nature too, and the benefits of being in nature are well documented. We are also reminded to focus on what we can control and what we need to let go of, like the weather.

One of my biggest "letting go" lessons in the garden was growing carrots. Bear with me. Carrots are a very temperamental crop—they want fine soil without stones that is free-draining. They want to be fertilized, but only at a particular time in their growth. And they take up to four months to mature—that is a lot of time taking up space in the garden while they grow. No matter what I did, my carrots were always twisted, split, and too fibrous to really enjoy. They were always disappointing and they always became soup. And then one day, after about three years of trying, I thought, "I'm done with carrots. I am not willing to put in the work it will take to have a decent enough result. I'm more willing to go to the store and buy carrots!"

Sometimes we focus too much energy on things that are not working, but when we become present to this, we realize they are not that important to us anyway. Growing incredible carrots had never been a life goal for me, so I let it go. When I stopped and thought about what I was willing to tolerate, I was not willing to tolerate temperamental carrots.

Another aspect of presence I have learned from the garden is that if we are not present things fail to thrive, and sometimes wither and die. It is the same in life: if we are not present to the people we care about, our relationships fail to thrive and eventually die. I have witnessed this happen in my own relationships and in other relationships between intimate partners, family members, and friends, where one person is watching the relationship die right in front of them and the other partner has no idea about this slow death, because they are not present. And this can be applied to other areas of our life too. If we are not present and growing in our work, our enthusiasm dies; if we are not carving out the time for creativity, our creativity dies.

There is nothing living that will survive if it is not being fed. This includes you and the things that are important to you. Ultimately, when we are not present to ourselves and the lives we are living, we either allow parts of ourselves to die or we are fertilizing parts of our lives that do not matter anyway.

Power Process 1

1. What practices do you have that allow you to be present?
2. In what areas of your life do you struggle to be present?
3. What are the effects of not being present?

Action: What one action could you take today to practice presence?

III.

THE POWER OF SELF-AWARENESS

Self-awareness is deeply linked to presence. We have to be willing to be present to who we are, what matters most to us, and how we want to contribute to this human family. At the age of nineteen I read a book by James Redfield called *The Celestine Prophecy* and it changed my life. It made me realize that I had more control over my life than I had ever thought possible. The book is an adventure story set in Peru, but it explores psychological and spiritual ideas as part of the character's quest for meaning. It was the book that opened up the doors of personal development and self-awareness for me.

Before reading *The Celestine Prophecy*, I had been raised to believe that you play the cards you've been dealt, and you do the best with what you've been given. I had no idea that you could actually create a life on your own terms, if you were willing to stretch and grow. After reading the book, I was hungry to know more about myself, to become more self-aware. Why did I do the things I did? Why did I think the thoughts I did? How could I grow into a person I would be proud to be? How could I make the most of my life?

As far as I am concerned, deepening your self-awareness is pivotal for personal development. Self-awareness allows us to confront the parts of us that hold us back, and it allows us to understand who and what matters to us—to celebrate our strengths and strengthen our weaknesses (if that matters). When we take the time to know who we are and can accept our full humanity, we are on the road to becoming self-aware.

Cultivating greater self-awareness is like embarking on a hiking adventure, but within ourselves. We become aware of our motivations, emotional triggers, fears, and desires. When you set out on a big hike you need to know what tools and skills you already have, and what tools and skills you need to learn and pick up along the way. What tools do you have that are too heavy? What sort of food is going to sustain you? Are you afraid of deep water, the dark, or snakes? What is the purpose of the adventure? Who will support you along the way?

In personal development, we explore questions that lead us closer to ourselves, to our power. And the answers to these questions enhance agency in our lives. What are my patterns of self-sabotage? What brings me joy? Who or what makes me anxious? Why? We begin to understand the paths we have traveled and the paths we have yet to take. Having this information, we know our next actions and the safety measures we need to put in place to have the most fulfilling experience of this hike called life.

We don't suddenly wake up "self-aware." Self-awareness is an ongoing adventure, with many twists and turns. It is an adventure that will last until you take your final breath.

There are many different ways to support a person's journey to becoming more self-aware: books, courses, coaches, and therapists can be a great place to start. My first life-changing commitment to a personal development journey started with Sivananda Yoga. My girlfriend at the time was training to be a yoga instructor and started teaching me in our little flat in Chiswick, London.

People enter yoga via many paths, and I believe that each path is perfect for the seeker at the time. Sivananda appealed to me because it is a full system of yoga, including physical postures, breathing, relaxation, diet, meditation, devotional singing, and acts of service for the community. I also loved that the practice involves a repetitive sequence of physical postures and breathing components. As humans we are governed by sequences—the sun rises and sets every day, and seasons change every year. We have sequences built into us. In practicing Sivananda Yoga, I became aware of the fact that coming from an unstable childhood, I found a profound safety in a reliable sequence. This reliability meant that I always knew what was coming next in the practice, which was calming and comforting for me.

Next, I started attending the local Sivananda Yoga center and loved the energy there. I loved what could happen to my mind and body in that room. Not long after, I decided I wanted to teach others to experience what I was feeling, so I headed off to Kerala in South India to train as a Sivananda Yoga teacher.

My experiences in learning to practice and teach yoga in India opened up another level of awareness for me. I learned that I was attracted to kind and openhearted people, people who were open to ideas different from the "normal" paths. I no longer wanted to be around closed-minded or mean-spirited people.

On returning to London, I taught yoga in Notting Hill for a few years. But although I enjoyed teaching, I learned that I needed yoga as a foundation for my life. The more I taught, the less I practiced, and that didn't work for me.

My next life-changing experience of personal development and self-awareness was doing The Landmark Forum, an intense three-day personal development course. Landmark is an international organization that focuses on personal and professional growth. The premise of the course is to look at the stories we tell ourselves about the experiences we have had through our lifetime. It doesn't ask us to question the experiences, but we are asked to question what we made the experiences—good or bad—mean and how these stories impact on our experience of life. At the time, I was five months pregnant. My husband, Emrys, had already completed the course and looked after our toddler, Benjamin, at home in Melbourne while I went to Sydney to participate.

The course was life-changing for me—I witnessed a power I had never seen before.

On the first day of the course, I sat in my chair facing forward with the two hundred or so other participants as our forum leader entered the room from behind us. When she stepped onto stage, the first thing I thought was, "Yes! A woman of color!"

She introduced herself. "Hello, my name is Gitanjali Kopikar."

Gitanjali commanded the stage. She was the first woman of color I had seen who commanded a room with a power that seemed to radiate from the inside.

The Landmark Forum is not for everyone. The course can be an extremely confronting and uncomfortable journey at times. You are asked to look at the choices you have made in your life based on the stories you have believed. You are asked to look at the less-than-charming aspects of your choices. Being questioned about your lived experiences can challenge the life you have created for yourself. This was clearly the case for the large, stocky man who stormed onto the stage and angrily let rip his feelings about the course to Gitanjali. He was aggressive and forceful in both his energy and his actions.

I was really scared of him. I remember freezing, like I couldn't catch my breath. To me, he was a grown-up version of Darren Page. I was scared he was going to attack Gitanjali in some way.

I underestimated Gitanjali.

After he finished his rant, she asked him questions that seemed to calm him and put him in a more thoughtful state. I cannot remember exactly what she said to this man, but I do remember what she "did" to him. She was able to meet his anger with questions that made him look deeper. She was present to his anger; she stood with him and everything he was feeling. She was not afraid. She suggested reasons why he might be feeling the way he did, she inquired, and she was curious. She was one hundred percent present to him and fully self-aware of herself and her role.

By the time he walked off the stage about twenty minutes later, he was a completely different version of himself. Something happened on that stage that transformed him from an angry man to a humbled one. He now had a level of self-awareness he didn't have before.

The Landmark Forum leaders are highly trained and experienced in what they do, but at that moment, it looked like magic to me. I remember thinking, "How did she do that? I want to be able to do that, to stand firmly in my power in a way that creates new worlds for people. I want to create a space where a person can let go of what is holding them back and experience other ways of being and operating in life."

That thought was influential to me, and it was the first seed planted that led me to becoming a coach.

What I saw that day was a woman of color, Gitanjali, who was able to meet the societal power of the White man in front of her as an equal. She did not try to have power over him in the same way he had tried to have power over her—with aggression and might. She had something more powerful: the self-awareness to know who she was, and that she was there to bring about *his* self-awareness and transformation. It was a defining moment for me, watching an unapologetic woman of color own her power and her leadership.

When I look back at this moment, I have a clear picture of the situation. His power had been given to him. But Gitanjali *built* her power.

Power Process 2

1. How do you practice self-awareness?
2. How can you deepen your self-awareness?
3. What is there still to learn about yourself?

Action: What one action could you take today to become more self-aware of your thoughts and actions?

Power Story

Meredith

I am the classic "doer" and I do not like to sit still for long. I have derived a significant amount of pride from achievements, whether that be from school, work, or other hobbies and pursuits. They have fueled my sense of worthiness. And for a long time I considered this to be just dandy.

I enjoy feeling accomplished and contributing to a greater good, and I also love working hard and being rewarded for my efforts. That is all okay, but the emphasis I was putting into these endeavors was at the cost of my real sense of self-worth. I was yet to feel the sense of calm and self-assurance I was sure existed for me.

Before my coaching sessions I would grapple with feelings of being "not prepared enough," and the self-doubt would really kick in. I can see now that my understanding of self-worth and inner belief was pretty basic.

Then, one evening—I know it sounds a bit clichéd—I was standing by myself preparing dinner and I had a full-on "Aha!" moment. Something just clicked, and in that moment, I realized that I had to choose to back myself. I had to choose to feel worthy. It would not come from anything external. That was my moment of self-awareness.

I had been dictated to by a cacophony of external voices for so long, but what I needed to do was really listen and be present to my own inner voice. I had been covering her up with what I "should" be doing. I had drowned out my voice.

After this "Aha!" moment, I became more critical of the decisions I was making. I started asking myself a simple question: "Why I am I choosing to do this?" By creating a habit of asking this question, I started to notice my patterns of behavior—particularly where I was choosing to please others to my own detriment.

I started making a list of all the activities I was currently doing and took some time to consider whether they were activities that served me. By gaining this sense of clarity, I was able to back myself and my decisions because I knew they were coming from me, rather than all the noise.

It took sitting in the quiet and being present to my own voice to realize for the first time that I am proud of who I am as a person rather than proud of the things I am doing. This process is ongoing, and I am learning new ways to bring in more reflection time that works for me.

I know there will be periods of time where my inner voice is diminished, but now I also know I can draw upon my sense of power through being present to that voice.

24 years old. Sports industry

IV.

THE POWER OF DELIGHT

Delight (noun): A cause or source of great pleasure.

As far as I am concerned, delight is a much-needed power in today's world.

Big Magic by Elizabeth Gilbert is one of my creative bibles. It is a book that gives everyone permission to create, regardless of what their inner critic might think. When I read *Big Magic* for the first time, I was struck by a quote the author shared from Jack Gilbert (not related): "We must risk delight." In fact, I scribbled it down in my journal straight away—firstly because I believe that delight is an important aspect of life, but also because the quote left me with a question. Why is it a risk to feel and express delight?

It was around the same time that I started diving deep into the work of Brené Brown, who writes in her book *Daring Greatly*: "Softening into the joyful moments of our lives requires vulnerability." I think it's because when we "risk delight" we are also risking disappointment. We risk giving ourselves fully to a feeling that exposes us, and we risk losing control.

Delight is experienced in the small moments, in spontaneous interactions with others, with animals, in nature, in solitude. Delight can happen at any time, but you have to be present to catch it.

In the first couple of weeks of the COVID-19 pandemic, when the situation was revealing itself to the world and countries were shutting down, there was confusion everywhere. Once we all realized the severity of the issue, the next response, for many of us, was fear and panic. I saw that play out in my own life in many ways.

When COVID-19 first hit, I was in the middle of training for an ultramarathon. Even though the marathon was canceled, I initially decided to keep up the training schedule. For me, when there is a lot of fear and panic around and within, structure is helpful.

Once the need for physical distancing was announced, cases were rising, and big events were being canceled, I found myself sobbing at a bus stop one day because of the immensity of what was going on in the world. I had to tell my teenage son that he could not go to a farewell party for six exchange students who were returning to France before the borders closed, one of whom had been living with us. The school knew the party had been planned and had asked the parents to stop it from happening because of the restrictions on social gatherings, so I had to break the bad news to my son and bear his disappointment.

On another night, I locked myself in the bathroom and cried because I felt my whole family was being mean to me! I can't remember exactly who was doing or saying what, but I felt less resilient than usual. Everyone was around *all the time*, and when you're an introvert, you notice. Once I had calmed down, I knew there was only one solution. Crumpets! So in the end I took myself to bed with toasted crumpets and enjoyed the warm feeling of a good hot chocolate laced with rum. If you have never tried hot chocolate with rum, you may find it delightful.

It seemed that everywhere I turned, inexperienced people were giving advice on how to get through a global pandemic. As a coach, I was experiencing a slight internal pressure about this, thinking that I would be expected to join the online fray and launch a product or give advice. But I didn't have advice to give:

one, because I am not an expert in navigating a global pandemic, and two, because I was going through it too.

As a business owner and leader, I knew I wanted to do something for others, but I did not want to do it from a place of fear. There was so much going on in the online space that it felt overwhelming. How was I going to lead in a time of fear and uncertainty? I decided to turn inward for a few days. I kept things simple. I ran, I hung out with my family, and I gardened, all the while trusting that a useful way to contribute would come to me. I wanted to respond, not react.

One morning, while out running, with the sun just rising above the trees behind me, I came to the thriving and bountiful market garden near my home. The sunflowers in the garden were in full bloom and as I ran toward them the sun suddenly hit one particular flower. I sucked in a mouthful of air and came to a sudden halt (unfortunate for the cyclist behind me), and as I stood there staring at this regal flower with the sun not only kissing it but illuminating its beauty, I said to myself, "What delight!"

And just for that brief moment, the turmoil of the world was gone. And that is when I knew: I wanted to contribute delight at a time when it felt like the world was closing in. I wanted to invite people to tap into delight. Moments of delight are small, but they are real and the spirit needs these real moments, especially when a weighty darkness has fallen.

This is when the Delight Diaries were born.

There is a question I like to ask myself before I begin any project (I stole it many years ago from entrepreneur and author Tim Ferriss, who writes about it in *Tribe of Mentors*): "What would this look like if it were easy?" And I went from there. I made a simple announcement to my Instagram followers saying that what I wanted to contribute during this time was to share moments of delight. I would share my moments, and reshare the moments they shared with me.

The Delight Diaries were very well received, with hundreds of people sharing their delights. And in sharing in each other's delights, we were creating more delight in the world. It was . . . delightful. Some of the delights shared were: dancing around the kitchen with children while cooking, dancing to jazz while eating watermelon, early morning ocean swims, time with family, tomatoes turning red, a walk in the sunshine, cuddles with pets, and, of course, baking.

The Delight Diaries got traction. A number of organization leaders contacted me to say they had been so inspired with the Delight Diaries that they were using the idea in their team meetings during the pandemic. In the team online check-ins, they would ask each team member what their current challenge was and what their moment of delight was that day.

To experience delight, we have to be present. Delight is very easy to miss. And yet it is those small moments of delight that build into larger moments of happiness, then into contentment and on to fulfillment. In some ways, we are more conditioned to be cynical than joyful, because being cynical does not carry the risk of disappointment. And just as it takes practice to become a cynic, it also takes practice to experience delight.

Let me ask you a question. If you were in a room full of cynics but one person was experiencing a moment of delight, sharing it with others in the room, who would you be drawn to? The cynical or the delighted? Who has the power in the room?

We are inherently attracted to the power of delight.

We are inherently attracted to the light.

Power Process 3

1. Do you struggle to allow delight into your life?
2. What brings you delight?
3. How could embracing delight in your life shift things for you?

Action: What one action could you take today to add more delight to your day?

Power Story

Jessica

The power to take responsibility for my own joy in life required a little more motivation than I'd thought. To be honest, if you had told me ten years ago that I would need a push to do the things I love, I would probably have laughed—a lot! You see, I thought I already had delight in my life. It was quite natural for me to take off on an adventure, and I would focus energy and attention on myself.

But recently I'd found myself falling into the trap of the daily grind, showing up in a high-pressure job, giving it all I had during the week, then spending the little spare time that I had on the couch watching the latest Netflix drama with a glass of wine in hand and Uber Eats on the way! This was reinforced by a husband who is, for want of a better word, a homebody. He has a high-stress job also and his way of looking after himself is time spent at home in a safe, peaceful environment.

This combination led to a great deal of resentment on my part—I was constantly suggesting that we go hiking, climbing, swimming, but at the same time I found myself feeling too exhausted to organize it and drag him along, or to find someone else to go with me. I got more and more frustrated as the days went by. It really all came to a head for me while on a skiing trip last year, booked in a desperate attempt to fill the void. I was sliding down the mountain at full speed and screaming out loud to myself, "I feel alive!" And I thought, "Okay, so you can't do this every day, but it's time to figure out how to be in your body and present without hurtling down a mountain!"

So I signed up to listen in to an online session with Kemi. Through coaching, I soon came to realize there was only one person who could line up the adventures and excitement I needed—me—and that might mean doing these things alone. I realized that I had been waiting for someone to organize an adventure and take me along with them. Despite the fact that in my work I am a natural leader, when it came to my social life, I was a devoted follower. I recall feeling shocked about this when it dawned on me, but the more I explored it, the more it made sense.

But the thought of joining a group or seeking out people who might enjoy similar adventures to me filled me with horror. The clarity really came when I reviewed my core values and landed firmly on adventure and community being integral to my happiness. Once you know what is most important to you, the gaps in your world are glaringly obvious and the power to fill them up is in your hands.

So eleven years after declaring I would take up my childhood love of singing again, I actually got a singing teacher! In one of my first lessons we sang opera in silly accents and my belly ached from laughing, my face hurt from smiling, and somewhere in there I made some music that filled me right up to the top.

35 years old. Head of product, retail

V.

THE POWER OF EMPATHY

Empathy (noun): The ability to understand and share the feelings of another.

Empathy often gets confused with sympathy, but they are very different. And if you are the person receiving the empathy or the sympathy, you can feel the difference.

Empathy says: "I may not have experienced your circumstance, but I understand and acknowledge your feelings." Empathy connects people.

Sympathy says: "I feel sorry for you." Sympathy disconnects people.

I have been blessed to be in the orbit of incredible female entrepreneurs who are true collaborators and embolden each other's work. One of these women is Julie Parker, the founder of Beautiful You Coaching Academy. I had spoken at one of Julie's events but this was our first one-on-one meeting. We met at a café called Soul Sisters. Many years later, it is still our meeting place. There's no mistaking why a place called Soul Sisters Cafe is where we first got together and where we continue to meet all these years later—Julie and I got on instantly. Not only did she have a deep reverence and respect for women, she was also straight talking and bloody hilarious.

Although it was our first meeting, by the end of it we had basically created a yearlong group coaching program called The Sovereign Collective (TSC). It was a group coaching program that involved four full-day, in-person workshops over the year.

In each workshop, based on a season, Julie and I would coach, facilitate, teach, and hold space for sixteen female entrepreneurs at various stages in business. TSC was a gift. It defined success for me—I was doing what I wanted to do, with whom I wanted, where I wanted, and for as long as I wanted to.

Once the collective was over, Julie and I once again descended on Soul Sisters to debrief. What did we want to do next? We decided that we would run a women's retreat together in Bali. This was for 2020, so you know what happened to that retreat.

But before COVID-19 derailed our plans, Julie's designer was tasked to do the branding for the retreat. Julie and I were both sent a folder of pictures of diverse women to choose from for the retreat sales page.

I had admired Julie from early in our relationship, but there was something she did before we formed TSC that deepened my respect for her. Julie had shared that she was in the middle of a "White Privilege" course and shared with me what she was learning about herself and the privilege she was afforded based purely on her skin color.

Never had I met a White person who would take themselves on in that way, digging deep into their privilege and biases in regard to race. I knew this course had been life-changing for Julie, and because of it, she started making changes. She started with completely rebranding her Beautiful You Coaching Academy materials and marketing to be more inclusive and diverse, and began using her voice to speak out, even when it made others uncomfortable and angry.

A few weeks after we had both chosen the pictures, we received the first draft of the sales page. The header had the name of the retreat, my name, Julie's name, and just one picture—a solo Black woman, looking up to the sky. It was a beautiful picture.

And my first thought? "I hope that White women feel invited."

And there it is. There is a part of me that wants to justify this thought, but I am not going to. What I will say is that my next thought was, "I wonder how many White people think 'I hope that Black women feel invited' when they do their own marketing."

When Julie and I met next, I shared my first thoughts with her and her response was, "That is what internalized racism looks like."

And we both nodded silently, just letting that sit there. We both had tears in our eyes and gave each other a long, deep hug.

Because Julie had done the work to be present to her Whiteness, she could empathetically sit with my Blackness. Her response told me a few things that I want to share with those of you who are White but have not yet consciously explored the power of your Whiteness:

1. Julie was able to be present to my Blackness because she had done the work to be present to her Whiteness.

2. Julie was able to be present to what I was feeling without trying to fix, diminish, or gaslight the reality of my response—she had true empathy.

3. Julie's ability to be present to me and with me meant that I knew she and I would be walking alongside each other for many years to come.

As a Black person navigating White spaces, you know when you have found your true allies. Your allies can be fully present to you and your experiences regardless of their level of comfort or lived experience.

The sad reality is that many of us who live as minorities spend a lot of time making sure that the majority is not upset by our presence, by our words, by our difference. In doing so we only offer a shadow of who we are and what we have to offer. And many in the majority have no idea that we do this as a way of surviving these spaces. I am still unpacking the reasons behind the brakes that have been put onto me by others and the brakes I have put on myself because of my race and gender. As the years have passed, I have become less and less concerned about the comfort of others while enduring my own discomfort. I am now just as concerned about my own comfort.

There is the aspect of presence that includes being deeply present to yourself and others, and there is the aspect of presence that represents being seen.

Before the pandemic, I was due to speak at an event headlined by Tony Robbins. The topic I chose to speak about was "The Five Principles for Self-Leadership." It was for a mixed-gendered audience of three thousand people and it was an exciting opportunity. The event company was doing a lot of pre-marketing activity for the speakers, and I was sent a video that had been created by the media team as an introduction to my presentation.

As I watched it, my first thought was, "Where am I?" My actual image was at the start of the video, but the other images in the video contained few to no women of color. And where diversity *was* shown, the diverse people were not in leadership roles.

I did not want to be a woman of color standing onstage talking about "The Five Principles for Self-Leadership" with no women of color presented as leaders in the video.

I knew I had to point this out. I sent Simon, the video editor, an email sharing my concerns about the lack of representation and asked for the video to be amended to reflect greater diversity. The video that landed in my inbox four days later was a 180-degree about-face and it was moving to watch. Now there were more women of diverse backgrounds than there were White women. Simon had run with my feedback, and this is the exact email I sent in response:

> *Hello Simon,*
> *I know we will chat tomorrow, but I wanted to let you know that the video you have just sent through has brought tears to my eyes. Thank you for listening to me and taking action on my suggestion. What you have created is powerful. If I had seen videos like this when I was a child growing up in the United Kingdom, I would have felt I was seen and that I belonged and that I could aspire. For all of us who walk in the shoes of the minority (whatever that is), seeing ourselves translates as belonging. Thank you.*

Looking at the dictionary meaning of empathy—"the ability to understand and share the feelings of another"—I cannot say that Simon, a White male living in Australia, *shared* my feelings about "not seeing myself." That was not his daily lived experience. But his empathy showed up in his ability to *understand*. He understood my request and took extensive action to make sure that I felt seen—and in doing so, every single person of color in that audience would have felt seen too.

I understand that our lived experiences dictate what we know, and I try to never make assumptions or judge the understanding of others. My intention is to lead with empathy.

Since living in Australia, I have leaned toward praising the organizations and companies that have done more than pay lip service to diverse representation in their marketing. I remember a sleepwear company that had one Black woman as the model for its whole campaign—not as a token—and I nearly fell off my chair. It's unfortunate that I was so surprised.

But now I also reach out to the companies I care about and believe can do better when it comes to diverse representation. When I reach out to a company I am giving them the opportunity to invite me in as a customer—because the reality is if they don't see me, I won't see them.

Power Process 4

1. How does your internalized racism show up?
2. Where did you learn your internalized racism?
3. How does this affect your empathetic responses?

Action: What one action can you take today to be more empathetic?

VI.

THE POWER OF THE MIRROR

My family and I were invited to South India in January 2020 by friends who have lived in the state of Tamil Nadu for over twenty years, and have supported a school, children's home, and mobile computer bus in a rural fishing village. (It was on this trip that I saw the Matrimandir, conceived by The Mother.) Before going to visit our friends' home in the village, I wanted to share Indian city life with my family, so we spent several nights in Mumbai and Chennai. I had spent roughly two months in South India training as a yoga teacher and traveling, and I was excited to experience it again with my family.

My husband and I like to experience travel in different ways. I enjoy arriving in a place and just walking around, meeting who we meet, eating what takes our fancy, and ending up where we end up. I have minimal interest in tourist attractions. I am not judging people who like to see the important landmarks and sights of a place, but most of these attractions leave me cold. My husband also loves to walk, but he is one of those people who enjoys seeing the important tourist attractions. He reads up on the history of places we are going and then wants to tell me all about them. But I don't want to be told: I want to experience a place. The only area that I will research is food. I want to know about the best places to eat, and with my background as a chef, I have a good radar for tourist nonsense when it comes to food.

Over the years we have reached a compromise. What we now do is make the tourist attraction the destination, but how we get there is a bit more of an adventure.

On our first day in Mumbai, we decided to walk to the Mani Bhavan Gandhi museum.

We were on a mighty trek that day, a sensory extravaganza for us all. India arrests you on first contact, no matter how many times you have been there.

As we were approaching the museum, I looked to my left and saw a young Black woman in her late teens with a group of White people. Our eyes locked, we smiled, and she ran over to me.

"Oh my God, it is so good to see you here!" she said as she grabbed my arms.

"Do you want a hug?" I asked.

"Yes! Yes!" she replied and we hugged hard, much to the surprise of her friends.

I asked what her name was after we'd ended our embrace.

"Henrietta," she replied. "You have no idea what it means to me to see another Black woman here in India."

"Yes, I do," I replied. "It's as comforting for me to see you as it is for you to see me. When I first came here twenty years ago I never saw another Black person. Because of the caste system here in India, where the darker you are the lower the caste, I received a lot of negative attention—a lot of staring and uncomfortable exchanges."

We chatted more and it turned out that she was from Sydney. What were the odds of meeting another Black woman in Mumbai who happened to live in Australia? She was in India with a school group.

"I am so glad to have seen you," she said.

"And me you," I replied.

As she returned to her friends, I heard one ask, "How do you know her?"

"I don't," replied Henrietta, "but I do. We know each other."

And as we walked away my youngest said to me, "Black code, Mum. So cool!"

My husband held my arm and then my hand, without a word. He knew.

If I had met me in India twenty years ago, I would have run into my arms too. This is the power of the mirror when you are a minority. We don't "know" each other, but, as Henrietta said, we know each other.

And when we see each other on the street, on the TV, in the boardroom, that sighting says to us, "I can belong here too. I need to see you here so that I can see myself."

Being a mirror as a minority is powerful—it changes people's lives. I first saw Oprah Winfrey on TV when I was fourteen years old and my first thought was, "I didn't know Black women were *allowed* to do that!" As a young Black girl, I had been told exactly what roles I was destined for—the worst being a drug dealer's girlfriend. If I really wanted to succeed, I could be a nurse. Of course there is nothing wrong with being a nurse—thank the heavens for nurses—but I was given two choices and I had no interest in either. When I saw a "mirror" in Oprah, I didn't want to be her, but seeing her opened up a whole new world of possibilities.

If you are in a minority or a marginalized community and you are striving to be more than you have been told you can be, remember that on the days when you question yourself, or the journey seems too hard, there will be someone who looks like you who will see you. Seeing you could change their life—not because you mentored them, or even spoke to them, but because they saw you. You are their mirror. What a gift.

The power of the mirror is why it is so important that organizations have abundant diversity within the workplace. We are in a time where you can no longer say, "We have tried but . . ." If you do not have diversity within your workplace, you are not trying hard enough. You may need to invest time and money to work out what is missing and ask, *Why are we not attracting diver-*

sity? I promise you there are people of all colors, class levels, ages, physical abilities, and ethnicities who want to work in every industry. Do the work to attract them, find them, support them, and create structures to empower them. No excuses.

Do the work so we can all see ourselves in the places we want to be.

Power Process 5

1. What "mirror" is most important to you?
2. Who or what do you need to see to feel that you belong?
3. Who are you a mirror for and why is this important?

Action: What one action could you take today to acknowledge and thank your "mirror" person or people?

VII.

THE POWER OF THE PAUSE

There is much to be said about taking the time to feel, think, reflect, and review. To pause. But to pause can be challenging. Everyone who meditates knows how hard it is to pause, but we also know the power of that pause.

Pausing gives us the space to acknowledge what is going on, and once we know what is going on, we can then respond instead of react.

Reacting rather than responding is a recurring topic with my clients. In the moment that something happens, we all tend to think that reacting immediately is the best course of action. If you are a paramedic or someone is in a medical crisis, it may be that immediate action is generally the best—although I learned from a senior traffic police officer who has attended many fatal roadside accidents that when he arrives at an accident, he walks over very slowly: "As I am walking over, I am on high alert, assessing the situation, taking my time to respond so I can make the right choices. If I rush, I might miss something."

My theory is that it's always worth taking the time to make a considered decision. If it turns out to be the wrong decision in the end, at least it was a considered decision, and you gave it the respect to invest the time.

When working with clients, especially leaders who are constantly making decisions, I've noticed that they often feel the need to respond quickly. They confuse the speed of their response with the response itself. They can feel the pressure to respond to any issues or requests in the moment, even if they don't have all the information they need to make the best decision. These leaders often feel ineffective and question their leadership ability.

This can also be an issue for mothers—our big mother hearts go in quickly, and we often react instead of responding, especially when it comes to judgments made by others on our mothering or judgments or accusations made about our children. These parenting situations are the ones where we need to take the time to respond instead of reacting, because our emotions are high.

I found myself in a situation where my youngest had hurt a classmate in Year Three. The boy had been offensive to a friend and "slandered" that friend (so much slander in Year Three) and my child reacted by lashing out at the offender. Of course, my child shouldn't have physically hurt him and was in the wrong, but was protecting a friend, and of course I was protective of my child. I didn't want this one incident to be a moment of negative judgment on their whole personality.

I received a call from the boy's mother shortly after and kept in mind something my mother-in-law, Cheryl, had told me years before: "When it comes to playground disputes, each parent will defend their child; each parent thinks their child is in the right."

When speaking to this mother I made sure to pause and be present to everything she said. I did feel the need to defend and react, but I wanted a conversation of resolution, so if we were both defending and reacting, we wouldn't get very far. I listened to her as it was her son who had been hurt. I knew I could react by saying that what her son had done was offensive and my child had only been . . . et cetera, but once again I knew it would not be productive.

So I asked questions. I asked her what her son needed to feel okay about what had happened. I think she was surprised by my responses. In these situations it is easy to have two "warrior mothers" going at each other, but if no one is attacking, there is nothing to defend. It changed the energy of the whole conversation.

The conversation was respectful, and it ended with an amicable resolution. I didn't need to be right. If I was right, she would have been wrong, and she wasn't wrong. We both wanted the best for our children and that was what we both kept front of mind.

When we experience the benefits of pausing, we are more likely to reach a decision that works. We are a lot calmer and more effective when we pause. Pausing also allows us to trust our decisions more, because we don't rush into making them.

And, as I said earlier, if it turns out to be the wrong decision, at least we can take comfort in knowing we took the appropriate time. Staying present to which issues need immediate action and which can wait enhances our leadership, our parenting, and many other areas of our lives.

Not everything requires an immediate response. In the pause, power can be built.

Power Process 6

1. In what areas of your life do you react, even if pausing would be a more powerful choice?
2. What are the effects of reacting instead of pausing?
3. How would pausing benefit you in your life and work?

Action: What one action can you take today that will allow you to pause?

Power Story

Maddy

Starting my own business when I was just sixteen years old meant that I became very good at faking it. I would pretend that I knew how to do literally anything I was asked about, and then go away, research it, and get it done by the required deadline. I felt like I could never say that I didn't know something. After all, why would someone trust me and donate funds to a not-for-profit organization run by a teenager, let alone a teenager who didn't know what she was doing? The self-doubt was real.

This worked for the first eight years of running my business. I had managed to convince enough people that supporting the initiative was necessary and worthwhile, and we had raised just enough funds to hire our first real employee. All of a sudden, the employee had questions—and a lot of them. Next thing I knew, we were rapidly expanding, hiring our fifth, tenth, and then fiftieth staff member. I have never felt more out of my depth.

I was experiencing staff and culture challenges and I couldn't wing it through them. My team was questioning my decisions, talking back to me, and going off on their own paths, resulting in increased expenses and a growing list of mistakes. I often wondered if maybe I wasn't the right person to run the organization anymore. I felt like a failure ninety-nine percent of the time.

When I started receiving coaching, I was at a point in my leadership when I was ready to throw in the towel. I hated myself and felt anxious going to work each day. In one of the very first coaching sessions, we discussed the difference between reacting and responding. In my state of heightened anxiety, I had become a very reactive person. Each jab my team gave to me, I gave one right back. And because they expected a level of maturity and professionalism from me that I wasn't giving them, their reactions often made me feel diminished.

I slowly started to implement a practice in every aspect of my life. When something happened that took me by surprise, whether it was a comment, an action, or a new opportunity, I took three long, deep breaths. If I was then clear on how to respond, great! If there was still a voice in my head that wasn't sure, I replied with, "Let me think about this and come back to you." Easy, simple, and life-changing.

I have implemented this practice of pausing not only in my work life but in my personal life too. It helped me out of an emotionally abusive relationship, and helped me to navigate a year where our whole organizational model had to be flipped on its head. This practice has helped me to realize that I am the right person to be where I am right now. It is a power that no one can take away from me.

I am now a leader who is tuned in to my staff and deeply understanding of how they react to challenges in the workplace and what this means for team capacity, team culture, and job satisfaction. I'm a stronger leader and I can steer this ship that is a lot bigger than me.

29 years old. Founder and CEO, not-for-profit

In summary

Our power is built in our ability to be present. Presence can be confronting, because if we are present, we can't escape ourselves or others.

Presence builds true empathy, because we have to be able to sit with the lived experiences of others without trying to fix them or "make them better."

Presence builds self-awareness. We must take the time to understand who we are, who we have been, and who we want to become.

Being present to all of your feelings is more powerful than walking around with half of yourself hidden from yourself—in this situation, not only do you not belong to yourself, it also means others can't find you. How can we be accepted as whole humans if we only show a part of who we are? In being fully present, you experience being fully human.

As women, our ability to be present to ourselves is trained out of us so that we can service the needs of others. Being of service is wonderful, but we must be present to who we are, what we need, what we want to give, and what we have to give (and remember, the last two are not the same).

Our ability to be present informs our capacity for empathy, self-awareness, delight, the mirror, and the pause. Gitanjali embodied self-awareness. Her ability to be present to who she was created the opportunity for someone else's self-awareness. Julie was present to her conditioned response to racism, which enabled her to be empathetic toward my experiences. Henrietta was present to the relief she felt when she saw me, her mirror, which made her feel less "other." I was able to be present to that one brief moment of the sun kissing a sunflower—a moment of pure delight—so I shared that delight with others.

Presence expands our growth and is an enabler of further meaningful qualities. Once we unlock presence, it opens up how we experience ourselves and others in the world.

Presence is power.

Part 3

OWNERSHIP

"If I didn't define myself for myself, I would be crunched into other people's fantasies for me and eaten alive."

Audre Lorde

I.

O IS FOR OWNERSHIP

Ownership is the ability to integrate all parts of ourselves. As we explore our stories—those we have lived, those we are told, and those we have created—we take full ownership of who we have been and who we are becoming.

What does it mean to have ownership of ourselves?

It means that we can accept all aspects of who we are, our light and our shadows. Together, light and shadow form a whole picture.

It means that we take full control of our stories, what has happened to us, what others have done to us, what we have done to others, and what we have done to ourselves. Because there are many ways we can give away ownership of our lives.

Ownership of ourselves, including our flaws, aspirations, successes, and failures, brings one of the securest forms of power. If we own who we are—our complete humanity, with all its contradictions—then our humanity can never be used against us. We can instead use our humanity as a form of owning our power, and in doing so we allow others to step into their power too.

One of the strongest representations of ownership in the twenty-first century is Tarana Burke's #MeToo movement. Although #MeToo was started so Tarana could support and work with young Black victims of sexual violence, it soon became a global space where anyone could share their experience of sexual abuse, and take ownership of that part of their story.

When we take ownership of every part of our lives, we move into the driver's seat. We are no longer the passenger in someone else's vehicle, on someone else's journey, hoping we will end up where we want to go. Instead, *we* look at where we have been, where we are now, and what we need to take us to where we want to go. If we can understand and own the map of our lives, we have ownership of the journey and who gets to come along for the ride. We have agency in taking the next turn—or if we want to turn the car around and go in a completely different direction, we can.

Some people will jump out of the car if the direction changes, or you may ask people to get out, thanking them for traveling with you this far, as you continue to drive toward your destination, if you have one.

The following stories shine a light on the qualities we must own within ourselves to be unapologetically ourselves. Our heritage, our imprints, our beliefs, our ability to let ourselves be seen, and the agency we grant ourselves in our lifetime all build our power. You will also read the Power Stories of Jeanette-Margaret, Fowsio, and Bridget, women who have taken ownership of themselves in different but powerful ways. May their stories give you the power to own any parts of your story left unclaimed.

II.

THE POWER OF HERITAGE

Due to Western perceptions of Black women who have a voice as "the angry Black woman," for a long time I was too afraid to speak. It was a label I lived under (not with) and it did a great job of making me feel small. I hid myself away so that others would feel comfortable around me. I worked hard at being a "good girl."

But sometimes it didn't matter how good I was trying to be—I would still be called intimidating. "Intimidating" is defined in the *Oxford English Dictionary* as "having a frightening, overawing, or threatening effect." I have never been told I am intimidating by another person of color. For some people, the notion of a Black woman, with or without a voice, is intimidating. I have been called intimidating because I walked into a room and I hadn't even said a word.

Over time, I have come to realize that there is a difference between being intimidating and someone feeling intimidated, especially when there is racial bias in play.

Although I went to school in Nigeria for a brief period as a very young child, I have no memory of this time. But when I was in my mid to late teens, I went to Nigeria with my final set of foster parents because my foster father had a work placement there. On that trip, a galvanizing moment occurred for me when we stepped off the plane into a wall of intoxicating heat to see a row of Nigerian women waiting for their friends and family. Some of the women were in Nigerian dress, others in Western dress, and some wore a mixture of both. They were looking excited, searching for loved ones walking off the plane. Others were laughing and chatting together. I remember thinking, *People think I'm intimidating? They should stand in the presence of these women . . . what power!* In my eyes they had full ownership of themselves, which was powerful.

I have no idea what was going on for these women internally, but their external presence could not be denied. Some people may have found them intimidating but I found them reassuring. I also felt proud. I thought, *This is where I come from. These women are formidable in their presence; there is no apology from them for their stature, their grace, or their power.*

And then I thought, *What if I no longer apologized for this part of me? What if I stopped being good all the time? What if I could be more than good? What if I could stand tall and proud as a Black woman in the White world I live in?* Imagine all the other ways I could be in the world. Suddenly, *good* felt very limiting. And over time I realized it wasn't "niceness" I was displaying anyway: it was a survival reaction to trauma.

In that moment I wanted to give myself permission to stand in and own the power of the lineage of women I came from, but I did not yet feel safe enough. Having Nigerian heritage means I come from a country where women were, before colonization, the rulers of the money, the home, and the field. Yet being raised in the patriarchal United Kingdom's model of power, I'd seen that women were expected to be meek and submissive. There was no sudden transformation on that trip, but a seed was planted, and the image of those women is as clear to me now as it was twenty-seven years ago.

At primary school I was always called racist names—"coon," "nig-nog," "wog," "Blackjack," to name a few. The only one I felt I could refute was "Blackjack." I would stand up for myself by saying, "I'm not black, I'm brown. And my name's not Jack, it's Kemi. So call me 'BrownKemi.'" Of course, they never did.

Even at this young age, although clunky, I was trying to own myself. But I took *full* ownership of my heritage shortly after that visit to Nigeria. I began to own what I had been raised to believe was bad about me. I started telling everyone, without shame and without pause, "I am a Black woman."

In my younger teen years, I was cast in a hip-hop music video to be filmed in London, through a connection from the weekend drama classes I had been attending. It was all very thrilling—I was to be an extra with one line of dialogue.

I remember traveling on the train to London, feeling a little nervous, but more excited to be surrounded by people who looked like me, to be in a group and not stand out. To belong. I was so excited to be with "my people."

I sat in the green room with the other cast members, listening attentively to the instructions we were all being given about how the day would go. I asked a question and I saw a few people whispering to each other after I spoke. I didn't think much of it, but I did start to feel "something," an unease.

The filming began. There was a lot going on—there is so much choreography in a music video that there's not a lot of time for chatting. Then we broke for lunch and I walked over to a group of people who were having a conversation.

But when I introduced myself, someone said, "You don't sound Black, you sound White."

And someone else added, "A proper coconut."

I didn't know this at the time, but a "coconut" is a term used to describe someone who is Black (or Brown) on the outside but "White on the inside," implying that they're not connected to their culture.

My brain didn't compute, but my gut did. I felt sick. Weren't these "my people"? Wasn't I supposed to belong to them? I had thought for so long that I just needed to be with other people who looked like me; that way, I would feel like I belonged to something. I knew in that moment that they didn't feel I belonged to them. And deep down, I didn't feel it either. The reality was, they were Black people (and unlike me, had probably been raised in their Black families) living in London—an urban environment with its own dynamic mix of African and Caribbean cultures. I was raised in Kent, known as the "Garden of England" because of its abundant orchards. I grew up surrounded by farm paddocks and living with White families. I knew more about the harvest time of apples than I did about Black culture in London. I knew more about country-and-western music than I did about jazz or hip-hop.

Traveling home on the train, trying to understand what had happened, I made a deal with myself. I made an internal declaration: "If I don't belong in a White world, and I don't belong in a Black world, I'm going to belong to myself. I'm going to be Kemi first."

From then on, instead of searching outside myself for a sense of belonging, I was going to go inside. I was going to learn how to piece all of these parts of me together. I would have the courage to own myself.

I chose to stop feeling ashamed when Nigerian people asked me why I didn't speak Yoruba, my parents' native language. Instead of feeling like a "bad girl," smiling and hoping the accusations would end soon, I started saying, "I was not raised with my Nigerian family." When White people would expect me to like "Black music" (whatever their definition of that was), I would proudly say, "I love lots of music, including Dolly Parton and musicals."

How I choose to identify, the languages I do or do not speak, the music I do or do not like, the food I do or do not cook, is not up for scrutiny from others. Their "measurement" of me is not as important as how I measure myself.

Now I own my Nigerian heritage and I own my English culture. I have pride in both and I can honor that pride in whatever way I choose.

There is power in owning our heritage, on our own terms.

Power Process 7

1. What negative beliefs, if any, do you have about your heritage?
2. How have these beliefs played out in your life?
3. How has holding these beliefs affected your power?

Action: What one action could you take today to honor your heritage on your own terms?

Power Story

Jeanette-Margaret

While I might appear to be the model of middle-class education with an academic family, that is where the clarity ends: being adopted does that. Throughout my life, I inherently believed I was powerless. My birth mother had relinquished me. I had a constant deep-seated fear that if I did not oblige, behave, cheer up, confirm, achieve, be less sensitive, or succeed, I might be given back again and "returned to sender."

So I put my head down and made sure I continued to prove why I was worthy to remain in the world.

Recently my senior corporate leadership role, where I had up to eighty direct and indirect people reporting to me, expired within the budget constraints of yet another restructure. I woke up realizing that I too had expired, along with a frequent-flier points balance that reflected far too many hours in seat 6C.

Along with expiration came exhaustion and exasperation. How could it be that during the preceding five years of being a corporate traveler, I knew the flight attendants' names but had not a single person to call a close friend?

During a protracted COVID-19 lockdown and with no "bubble buddy" options, I turned inward. I devoured a year's worth of my personal library, acquired in various airport layovers. I also watched delicate documentaries and mindfully completed hamster laps on the nearby cricket pitch, unable to venture to other terrains due to the three-mile restrictions on movement. Lockdown became an intensely personal sabbatical, and with each chapter

I read, documentary I watched, and lap I completed, I bravely circled closer and closer to the inner me.

Introspection and self-work on vulnerability allowed my ideal future to become clear. Through this dialogue I was able to eliminate self-defeating beliefs and the negative labels of being discarded trash.

A few months later, two career opportunities presented themselves. Both were aligned to the glorious portfolio career that I was now aiming for. Both options were phenomenal. I knew that I had the ability to own my situation and the implications of this watershed decision. It is said that through the hard choices we make, we can become the authors of our own lives. I made a choice, and by at last backing myself I regained ownership of what it meant to be me.

Owning the narrative looked like something I had never done before. At one of Kemi's retreats, she asked us to write a poem where each line began with the words "I am." The first line included my birth name, the last line my adopted name. The nine lines were a personal progression from the old, tired, and overplayed narrative to a new one. When I read the poem to the group, no one knew that I had never uttered my precious birth name in public before. My heart beat loudly.

By owning that most basic of human elements—my name—the mental mists cleared to a brighter light. And that is where the power lies. Reading the poem out loud was exceptionally difficult. Yet owning my name has given me immeasurable power.

48 years old. Vice president, industrial technology business

III.

THE POWER OF IMPRINTS

Imprint (noun): A mark made by pressure; a mark or figure impressed or printed on something.

As a speaker, one of the topics I am most often asked to talk about is called "Women and Worth." It is one of my favorite keynotes to deliver. Once I have been introduced to the audience, I like to share with them what I do as a coach and how my work supports leaders. Then I ask the question: "Who in this room considers themselves to be a leader?"

In a room of two hundred women, maybe a quarter will raise their hands. Sometimes the event is an actual leadership event, which means they are there because their organizations see them as leaders, but still only a quarter of the women see themselves in this way.

I then ask everyone to close their eyes. I let them know that I will be saying three words to them and I want them to be aware of the first images that come to mind. I ask them not to edit what they see.

Once everyone has closed their eyes, I say the words in quick succession: lawyer, professor, doctor.

I ask the women to open their eyes and ask them, "Who did you see?"

And the response is always the same.

A White, middle-aged man.

Even if we know better in our conscious state, our imprints

run deep. It was certainly imprinted on me that lawyers, professors, and doctors were definitely the jobs of White men.

Once, a woman raised her hand and said, "This is very strange to me, because I am a doctor and even I saw a White male first!"

Although we all laughed, the imprints we have regarding who gets to do what job in this world are limiting and oppressive. I remember one woman being shocked by the image she saw. Her sister is a lawyer, and she did not see her; the person she grew up with and loves is a lawyer, but she still saw a faceless White man. In the first few years of my husband becoming a barrister (yes, I am married to a White lawyer), he would come home and tell me about the outcome of a case and say, "The judge . . ." and the first image I had was a White man in a wig, even though we personally know female judges, and hardly any lawyers wear wigs anymore.

Mary Beard, professor of classics at the University of Cambridge and author, says this very well:

> *If we close our eyes and try to conjure up the image of a president or—to move into the knowledge economy—a professor, what most of us see is not a woman. And that's just as true even if you are a woman professor: the cultural stereotype is so strong that, at the level of those close-your-eyes fantasies, it is still hard for me to imagine me, or someone like me, in my role.*

When I share with the audience the Oxford Dictionary definition of power—"the ability to do something or act in a particular way"—I ask, "Do you have the ability to do something or act in a particular way?"

Everyone raises their hand.

So I ask again, "Raise your hand if you consider yourself a leader," and this time, about three-quarters of the room put their hands up.

We can't underestimate the effect of the imprints we have around power and leadership. We have to unpick the social and familial overlays before we can lay claim to our agency and power. When I coach female leaders, a lot of the work we do is unpicking why they do not see themselves as worthy of being a leader. They may have the office and the title, but their internal dialogue does not match their external circumstances.

This is important because as women we have opportunities now like never before, but if we do not step into those opportunities with the belief and confidence in our right to be there, we will not be able to make the difference so many of us want to make. Our imprints are real, and if we do not actively pick them apart, they will be our downfall. This is why it is so important for women to come together and share these experiences, because we are not alone. Most of us have some form of conscious or unconscious imprints. Sharing them with each other diminishes their *power over* us.

We cannot afford to undo the work of so many women before us. They got us to where we are today, and if we do not "undo" ourselves and our imprints, we will undo each other.

I hope one day soon to stand in front of an audience of women and say, "Lawyer, professor, doctor," and hear that people saw all ethnicities, all abilities, and all expressions of gender. Some women in the room will still see the White man, which is okay. White men can still be leaders, but they are not the only leaders we want to see. We want different leaders, because more than one type of person can lead.

Diversity in leadership is for the collective good. We all need to see ourselves in all the places decisions are being made.

We all have the ability to lead, if we want to lead. But to do so in a powerful way, we have to own who we are and what we bring to the table. We must take ownership of the imprints that have held us back along the way and may still be holding us back, so we can take full ownership of our leadership.

There is no quick fix for any of this unlearning, but the awareness of what has been imprinted upon us is a powerful first step. It takes us from "I'm not a leader" to "I question if I can be a leader, and that I lack confidence, because there are no models around me. But that doesn't mean I am not leadership material."

It is why the mirror in "Presence" is so important. Find your mirror for how you want to live and lead and you'll know it can be a reality for you, even if you don't yet know how. And if you can't find a mirror, be the first, and you'll *become* the mirror. You will be the mirror who undoes the limiting imprint for someone else.

Power Process 8

1. What imprints do you have about leadership?
2. Where did these imprints come from?
3. How have these imprints affected your work and career aspirations?

Action: What one action could you take today to unpick your imprints?

Power Story

Fowsio

My journey in taking responsibility and ownership for my personal development and growth has been an amazing experience. I have learned how my negative beliefs were affecting my life.

Before, I was lacking in confidence, almost always doubting myself. My limiting beliefs included not believing that I had the capability to do what I wanted. I was so fearful of failure and rejection, especially when it came to creating my own business, that I would always ask others what their thoughts were on a business idea I had, in order to get their approval. I would allow their beliefs to take over my mind and then I would lose momentum, procrastinate, and get stuck. Delaying things and not taking action made it even harder.

I remember sharing my passion and business dream with my husband and his feedback was, "Don't waste your time and money on this obsession—concentrate on your job and the children, it is enough." In some ways it is enough—we have a child with additional needs who is four years old. I come from a traditional culture, and I kept telling myself that people would come around one day, understand my decision, and embrace it. I would try to get their approval by sharing some of my learnings regarding creating an online business and my newfound passion for real estate. But deep down I realized that I wasn't going to get approval. All I was hearing was, "Don't do it—you are wasting your time, money, and effort."

One of the challenging decisions I've made is to only share my personal development with the people who support me. For me, this is bold and brave, and I am proud of myself for this wise decision. One of the people who continues to believe in me is Mum. She is the best: very strong and loving, and she is the one who encourages me.

I will also continue to explore my newfound passion for real estate. I am hoping one day to be the best buyer's agent in the country—a proud Black hijabi woman expert in a real estate agency in Australia.

I am enough, and I can follow my dreams and passions.

42 years old. Director and founder, childcare business

IV.

THE POWER OF TAKING UP SPACE

I believe there are two types of people in the world: those who love musicals and those who hate them. I have never met anyone who was so-so about musicals—you are either in or you're out.

I am in. I even told my husband that the first full-length movie our children would watch was going to be *The Sound of Music.* Even with its strong patriarchal overtones, rigid gender roles, and other offenses in the musical, the songs are *so* good and there's Julie Andrews—and Christopher Plummer is so handsome.

I have even managed to bring musicals into my work. A clip from a rehearsal for the musical *The Greatest Showman*, based on the life of American showman P. T. Barnum and starring actors Hugh Jackman and Keala Settle, is a favorite. Keala has Maori, Pacific Islands, British, and American heritage, was raised in Hawaii, and went to school in Utah. On this particular rehearsal day in the clip, the musical director asks Keala to come out from behind the music stand, where she is singing, to claim her voice and space, because up until then she has been using the stand to hide behind it.

In the beginning of the song "This Is Me," when Keala starts to sing, she remains behind the music stand, singing gently, apprehensive. But as the song and its powerful lyrics progress, her voice begins to falter with emotion. Suddenly, she lowers the music stand and her voice becomes bolder. She steps into her voice, into the center of the rehearsal space, and, surrounded by her fellow actors and musicians, she sings her heart out.

As her ownership of the space and boldness in her voice

grows, so does the joy and engagement of everyone around her. Keala and the chorus sing in unison and the room is ignited. She is dancing and singing at the top of her lungs, commanding the space and pulling in everyone around her. Everyone is up on their feet dancing and singing. Not only does Keala give herself permission to own her space, but in doing so she gives every other performer in that room the permission to claim space with her. When she dares to be seen, *everyone* dares to be seen. All the voices come together and so do the stories, voices, wounds, and joys of everyone in the room.

Whenever I show this video, it has a deep impact on my workshop participants, and I shed a tear every time—not only because of the power of the lyrics in "This Is Me," but also in response to the gift of being let into the power of someone fully owning who they are and what they have to offer, when a woman claims her space and her voice without apology.

In an interview, Keala shared: "We're all the same as much as we're so different, and we should totally bask in that. We all have the same need to connect, and that will never go away, because we're human beings and we're alive. And it's in those connections that we can begin to realize that everyone feels like they're not right."

When we focus on our perceived flaws as an excuse not to show up in the world, we are perpetuating a destructive myth that only perfect is acceptable. We all want to feel that we are seen and understood by others with our beauty and our flaws.

Think about the people in your life you connect deeply with. Are they perfect? Do you know a "perfect" person? In reality, no one relates to "perfect." Can you imagine spending time with a perfect person? Personally, I would be incredibly bored.

It is our humanity that makes us interesting and acceptable. It is our humanity that enables others to connect with us in a meaningful and authentic way.

There is power in taking up space and being seen. There is power in allowing others to see you with all your human imperfections.

When we can honor imperfection in ourselves, we can honor imperfection in others.

Power Process 9

1. What perceived flaws do you need to accept in yourself?
2. What perceived flaws do you need to accept in others?
3. In what area of your life or in the way you lead do you need to stop hiding?

Action: What one action can you do today to take up a little more space?

V.

THE POWER OF BELIEF

Belief (noun): An acceptance that something exists or is true, especially one without proof.

Words play a monumental role in my life. They play a monumental role in all of our lives, even if we don't recognize it. The words we hear shape how we experience ourselves and how others experience us. Words have the power to build or diminish our power.

In the introduction to this book, I mentioned that the reason I have defined certain words throughout is because I had made assumptions about the meanings of some words and this led me to believe certain untruths, which ultimately led me to feeling powerless. What we believe about ourselves dictates the actions we do or do not take. Our beliefs steer us through life, so being conscious of them is powerful.

If we believe we have power, we will act very differently compared to when we feel we are powerless.

A White male CEO, a friend whom I respect immensely, once said to me, "It is the fact that you look the way you do, and do the work you do the way that you do it, that makes you so valuable to organizations like mine. You are walking into organizations and richly transforming them by being there in your power."

I don't share this to blow my own horn; I share this with you because I had never seen it that way. I had been taught that my color and my being had to be justified in some way. I believed that I would need to work very hard to make sure that people could see through the obstacle of my skin color. I believed that if I was amenable and likable enough, then maybe I would be "allowed."

In the past I spent a lot of my time and energy trying to make up for being Black. I knew from the age of five that my skin color was seen as an obstacle, something that would always be used by others to insult and belittle me. This led me to my belief that I would always need to compensate for my Blackness, which led to hiding parts of myself and not wanting to take up space.

Many years ago, a friend and colleague who is a well-regarded and respected leader in her field said to me, "I love your ambition."

I sat there stunned and a little offended.

She looked at me. "You seem offended?"

In that moment, I understood that I had always believed that "ambitious" was a dirty word for a woman to use to describe herself. If I had ever heard anyone say, "She is ambitious," it was in an unfavorable tone. Ambition equaled being deceitful and untrustworthy.

But this friend was someone I looked up to. She was ambitious herself and she was not deceitful or untrustworthy.

Sitting on the tram on my way home from that meeting, I remember thinking, "Am I ambitious?" As a lover of words, I looked up the meaning of ambition in the dictionary, to unravel it from what I had believed it meant.

> **Ambition** (noun): A strong desire to do or achieve something.

Where had I gotten "deceitful and untrustworthy" from?

> **Deceitful** (adjective): Guilty of or involving deceit; deceiving or misleading others.

Untrustworthy (adjective): Not able to be relied on as honest or truthful.

It was all tied up with a negative connotation of women and power that many of us have been led to believe, and then adopted as unconscious ways to diminish ourselves and each other. When I read the true meaning of ambition, in combination with someone I greatly admired telling me I was ambitious, I felt proud to be ambitious.

I *am* ambitious. I have work to do in the world and I want to make the most valuable and impactful contribution I can. If that is ambition, I'm in.

At this stage in my life, the lessons about my transferred beliefs were coming in thick and fast.

At a dinner party one night, another good friend said something about my intelligence.

I said to myself, "Intelligence?"

I tried to stay with the rest of the conversation at the dinner table, but internally I was feeling a little unsettled. Describing me as "intelligent" completely butted up against what I had been told about myself and what I had felt comfortable telling myself. How could I be intelligent if I had been in the lowest class in math at school? How could I be intelligent if I had not gone to college?

So once again, I looked up a word to see if my belief and the actual meaning were aligned.

Intelligence (noun): The ability to acquire and apply knowledge and skills.

Seriously? That's not what I thought it was. I adore applying knowledge and building skills.

And this is where I'd been tripped up:

> **Academic** (adjective): Relating to education and scholarship.

This friend of mine is next-level intelligent by anyone's measure—a barrister who excels at every level—so I could not brush off her words. I had to sit in the uncomfortable feeling that maybe I had been lied to, and that I had believed that lie. And in believing that lie, I had cut myself off from opportunities. I had believed something about myself that had restricted my view of what I was capable of. And how had this lie shaped my identity?

It was made very clear to me at school that not much was expected of me because first of all, I was Black (in an all-White school), and second, I was a foster child. Just the fact that I turned up to school was enough to blow some of my teachers' minds. I was never encouraged to excel, because in their eyes I was doing a good-enough job by turning up at school in the first place. They expected nothing more from me. On the one hand, this gave me the ability to count on myself, but on the other hand, it has sometimes been a lonely path, believing I had to do everything for myself.

We build beliefs over time, from either what we are told, what we are shown, or what we experience. Not all our beliefs are true. Taking the time to examine your beliefs about yourself can be a life-changing action.

And now I can proudly say: I am ambitious. I am intelligent. I can count on others, not just myself. And—as I've said before—I no longer have any interest in being a good girl.

Power Process 10

1. What negative beliefs do you have about yourself that hold you back?
2. Where do these beliefs come from? Who gave them to you?
3. Which beliefs do you need to let go of, and which ones will you choose to own?

Action: How can you reexamine your beliefs today?

VI.

THE POWER OF AGENCY

Having agency builds power. To have a feeling of agency means that we feel in control of our lives, as much as any of us can be, and that our thoughts, feelings, and actions are our responsibility. There are many ways in which we can ignite agency, and one way is in how we manage our personal narratives.

I do not want to be portrayed as "the poor Black foster child who made good." I have had to say this many times because people love this angle, including the media, journalists, and some speaking agents (a speaking agent is someone who acts on behalf of a speaker to find them speaking engagements).

When I first started speaking professionally as a coach, I consciously decided to share my childhood story because I know our stories connect us to each other. And because of my childhood experiences, it means as a coach I am able to "stand outside" of someone else's experiences, someone else's life. It was relevant to me being able to "enter into the lives of others," to observe and hear what was being said between the lines as a coach.

I also began to understand the power of listening to and sharing our stories.

But when and where I share my story is completely up to me, because it is my story. My childhood does not define me, although it has shaped me.

In the early days, when I was interested in working with speaking agents, this was always the angle many wanted to take. I love a rags-to-riches story as much as anyone else, but as a woman of color I need to be mindful of the subtle undertones. As

Roxane Gay, the Black writer, professor, editor, and social commentator, says, "Women of color are often exploited to write of tragedy and trauma; to cannibalize themselves to get ahead."

This has been my experience. I would have meetings with people and when they asked me about the topics I spoke about, the main focus for them was always the rags-to-riches angle—they knew how to sell me as a Black woman if I was "sharing my story." I knew that if I succumbed to how they wanted to sell me as "talent" I would not get to speak about the work I am deeply passionate about: women, well-being, and leadership.

Most of those meetings came to nothing.

If I had found a speaking agency that was willing to see beyond "my story," maybe I would have a great partnership with it today. I spent a few years trying to find—actually, let's be honest, "wanting to be chosen" by—a speaking bureau, because I believed that "real speakers" had agents. The problem with being represented in this way was that it put me in a place where I had no power or ownership of my own story, and that left me feeling powerless.

The role of an agent is to sell their client, and no agency knew how to "sell" me. So after a while I realized that I was going to have to be my own "agent" with my own agency.

What those experiences taught me was to have my own back and own my value.

After starting my business, I really wanted a mentor and was actively on the lookout for one. I'd met a very successful female business owner through various events I'd attended and we had several mutual contacts. Over time, as I got to know her, I asked if she would consider being my business mentor, and I was thrilled when she said yes.

In our first meeting, I was so excited and explained to her what I loved about speaking, and how I wanted to work with women in the areas of leadership and well-being.

Her response was, "You would be a great speaker on diversity."

I let her know that diversity was not what I spoke about, and that just because I was a "person of diversity" didn't mean I was an expert on diversity and inclusion. I told her that my areas of focus were women, leadership, and well-being. But she kept on insisting that she could get me a lot of speaking engagements if I spoke about diversity and my story. And I kept telling her that diversity was not my topic, and my story was not always relevant in the content I shared onstage.

She persisted. I clarified again. She was not listening. I became quiet. I nodded and smiled.

As I walked away, I felt deflated. She was a very inspiring and generous woman, but I knew that she was not the right mentor for me. She was trying to mold me into who she thought I should be, to speak about what she thought I should speak about as a Black woman.

Our stories are ours to share, when and how we choose to. I have been formed by my story, I have been wounded by my story, my power has been birthed of it. My story is mine to heal, to honor, and to hold.

What I do with my life—past, present, and future—is mine. What you do with your life—past, present, and future—is yours.

Don't let others define you or determine the course of your journey.

Power lives in having agency in your life.

Power Process 11

1. Do you allow others to shape you in a way that serves them but undermines you?
2. In what circumstances do you allow this to happen, and why?
3. What do you need to do to take your story back?

Action: What one action could you take today to take full ownership of who you are?

Power Story

Bridget

I remember when I trained as a chef and I was taught how to cut an onion. I always found it difficult to cut and knife work was never my strong suit. I didn't understand why I had to cut it that particular way. But I always thought to myself not to second-guess what I had been told. What did I know, anyway? Five years later I worked with a chef called Jenna who showed me the way she cut an onion—the traditional Lebanese way. It was practical and easy; Jenna said she didn't have time to mess about. I was dumbfounded that we could actually choose the way we wanted to do things.

For most of my life, I didn't do what I wanted to do. Instead, I did what I thought I should be doing or what I thought others thought I should be doing. I ignored my inner voice, or I didn't know how to listen to it yet.

It has taken a lot of work to recognize the stories I tell myself. These are some of things I've told myself:

If you say you are going to do something, you do it, otherwise it means you are lazy or letting people down.
In business you need to go big and hard and live the hustle life.
If you take a job, you need to stay in that job for at least two years.
You should take romantic relationships slowly and not get too excited, as it could all fall apart.
You always need to do the right thing by others, even if it means hurting yourself.

During coaching, I had to document the goals I wanted to achieve. One of these goals was to create video content for social media because, you know, that's what everyone should be doing with their business, right?

A couple of months into coaching, I started dreading our upcoming session. I had not done my first video for social media. Everything in my body was screaming not to do it. Why was I torturing myself like this? Was I doing the videos because I wanted to, or because I thought I should do them?

I realized I didn't want to do them, and I felt instantly relieved and the stress disappeared. I could do what I wanted to do. I felt in control and empowered.

Once I made this decision, the realization started to pour into other areas of my life. I was renting a kitchen I no longer wanted to be in. I worked a part-time job that I felt took away my time, mental energy, and focus from my own business. I had recently moved in with roommates instead of living with my new boyfriend, because I believed moving in too quickly with him was doomed to end in failure.

For a long time, I had been operating from a place of fear. Where would I find another kitchen? How would I resign from my job? How could I tell my roommates that I was ending my lease to move in with my boyfriend? And what if it went wrong?

Moving away from what I think I should be doing to doing what I want to do has been so liberating. I am bound to face fear again throughout my life, but I can confidently say that no matter what, I am and will always be okay if I truly listen to and believe in myself.

35 years old. Founder, food manufacturing business

In summary

Building power through ownership of ourselves is a choice we must make at some stage in our lives if we are to experience power.

It may seem easier to blame someone else for the stories you have been led to believe about yourself. It is easier to blame our parents, our family, our heritage, our culture, but blaming never changes anything: it is exhausting and takes away our agency.

The truth is, there are structural systems at play that negatively affect each and every woman in minuscule and major ways. But if we can own the power of these structures, we can then own how we interact with them, how we choose to navigate them—and where necessary, dismantle them.

When you embrace the heritage you were gifted (including the stories you have been told about why your heritage is not a gift—assimilation or colonization, anyone?), you add to a collective story of humanity.

When you examine the imprints you have about gendered roles within the workforce, you have the opportunity to change these limiting imprints.

When you become curious about your beliefs, you have the ability to let go of the beliefs that no longer serve you.

Taking full ownership of who you are gives you permission to take up space as your imperfect self, which gives those around you permission to be imperfect as well.

Having agency in your life gives you the power to direct your actions, and therefore your life, without apology.

Ultimately, if you can have ownership over your story, it can never be used against you.

Honor your story and it will honor you.

Part 4

WISDOM

"You better not compromise yourself. It's all you got."

Janis Joplin

I.

W IS FOR WISDOM

We all have an inner wisdom that has the power to direct us through our lives. Too often we give that power away, but if we learn to trust ourselves, our innate wisdom will lead us.

It is easy to believe that wisdom is only gained from age and experience. Yes, there is definitely a level of wisdom that builds up over time—our lived wisdom, built through our mistakes and our successes, the actions we took and the actions we didn't take. Personally, and as a coach, I have found that we sometimes gain more wisdom from our failures than we do from our successes. But there are other forms of wisdom too.

We also have inner wisdom. Some call it gut instinct, others call it intuition or the universe, and some call it by the name of their god. Wisdom can also live in what we know, what we see, what we experience, and what we feel.

There is also wisdom in what we choose, such as the mindset we choose to have. When I think about some of the stories of my life, it would be easy for me to be angry and blame the people who took away my power by their words and actions. But I have chosen to believe that the people who powered over me during my lifetime did what they did because they . . . did what they did. I now understand there's no way I could have responded differently. I felt powerless because at the time either I was powerless, or I believed I was. In choosing my mindset I have developed a form of wisdom—the wisdom of knowing that walking through life blaming, angry, and powerless is not a wise choice.

Having wisdom does not mean traumatic things don't happen to us, or that we don't make mistakes, or take a wrong turn: wisdom shows itself in how we respond to the trauma or the mistake, or correct the wrong turn. Sometimes there is wisdom in letting go of a situation, and sometimes there is wisdom in holding on. Sometimes there is wisdom in going it alone, and sometimes there is wisdom in asking for support.

Wisdom is not a defined set of actions that can always be taken no matter the situation. Wisdom requires us to respond in a way that serves individual situations, with past experiences giving us information, and future goals giving us direction.

The stories in this chapter will demonstrate the Power Principle of wisdom in different ways—the wisdom in forgiveness, having fun, using our voices, setting boundaries, and initiation. The Power Stories generously shared by Eranthi, Heang, and Louise present a variety of ways to trust and own different forms of wisdom.

There is wisdom in choosing how we want to experience life—not in spite of our circumstances, but because of our circumstances.

II.

THE POWER OF FORGIVENESS

The act of forgiveness benefits not just the person we are forgiving, but ourselves as well. If we spend time carrying around anger and bitterness, we squeeze out the space for delight, connection, and joy.

The wisdom of forgiveness allows deep reflection into how we want to live. And it allows the possibility of a new beginning.

Our ability to forgive others is also linked to our ability to forgive ourselves.

How do we forgive ourselves when we have hurt others? How do you forgive someone who has powered over you? How do you forgive yourself for giving your power away?

There are no easy answers to these questions. Sometimes it is a mindset shift. Sometimes it is tapping into our inner wisdom. And sometimes it is just a matter of time. Depending on the situation, we may need professional support to guide us gently into forgiveness in a safe and respectful way.

Is forgiving easy? Sometimes it is, sometimes it isn't. Sometimes it takes a moment. Sometimes it takes a lifetime.

The benefits of reaching and offering forgiveness are numerous, and combine to impact mental health in a positive way: we experience less stress, less anxiety, enhanced self-worth, and healthier relationships. Just as importantly, forgiveness enables us to move past a perceived wrong or injustice and offers a new beginning—including, possibly, a sense of freedom.

There is a saying often attributed to Eleanor Roosevelt, the longest-serving US first lady: "No one can make you feel inferior without your consent." While that might be true in one sense, it doesn't take into account the many structures in place to keep certain groups of people powerless. Standing up against power when you have grown up to believe you don't have any takes strength. And in those instances, if you do give your power away—with or without your consent—how do you forgive yourself? How do you find self-compassion for the situation in which you've found yourself?

I once worked with a woman in her early thirties who worked in the fashion industry. In one particular session, she told me her stress levels were high because she was visiting her parents that weekend. There was a lot of pressure from her parents to "find a man and have a baby." In fact, she often avoided visiting, because whenever she walked into the family home, her mother or father would always comment on her lack of a relationship, her lack of a baby, or her weight.

"You're getting fat," was her dad's usual greeting.

"If you were pregnant it wouldn't be so bad," her mother might say, with a look of disappointment.

But it was her father's words that were especially painful, because not only was he her father, he was also a GP. He was coming from a significant place of paternal and professional power.

When I asked how she felt when she heard these words she responded, "Powerless and unlovable."

She had never told her dad that it wasn't okay for him to speak to her like this. Her cultural upbringing included spoken and unspoken rules about daughters belonging to their fathers, and because her father had supported her education and her career—not always a given in her culture—she had thought she was okay with his comments. It could be worse, she figured.

Over time, she realized she was no longer okay with it. She started to realize that the critical voice inside her head wasn't hers—it was her father's. That voice was always telling her she wasn't good enough.

When she decided to talk to her dad, her words were simple and direct: "Dad, from now on I request that you never make comments about my weight to me again. I know you love me, but I need you to love me in a different way. I am an adult and I am in charge of my health and well-being. If I need your professional input, I will ask."

In the silence that followed as her father processed her words, my client said she could feel her heart pounding.

And then her father said, "Let's have a cup of tea." This was his way of saying sorry.

She was able to forgive her father. "I know he loves me and it's his way of saying he's worried about me," she said. "He was born into a patriarchal family, within a patriarchal culture, within a patriarchal world. I needed to ask him to love me in a different way because 'powering over me' was all he knew."

Even though she could forgive him, she wasn't so generous with herself. She knew it was wise to forgive him, but . . . "I can't believe that I didn't say anything to him before this," she said. "Why did I let him have so much power over me? I feel so stupid that I let it go on for such a long time. All this time I have felt awful about not wanting to visit them and I should have said something earlier."

She had such a generosity for her father, and understanding why he did the things he did was the gateway to her forgiveness of him. I asked her questions that gave her the space to show herself the same generosity.

"Can you forgive yourself?" I asked. "You have forgiven your father, but can you forgive yourself?" I gently reminded her that as women who are raised within a patriarchy, we don't learn to hold our own power. That is the point and the power of the system.

Forgiving herself for not knowing she could ask to be loved in a different way gave her power. Her power came not only in forgiving him, but also in forgiving herself.

You may find yourself in a similar situation as you work through this book. You may be reminded of times when you gave your power away. It may have been your only choice in the circumstance, but when you play it back you find yourself filled with "woulda, coulda, shoulda" conversations. Instead of marinating in what could have been, practice forgiving yourself. Trust that there was no other way to respond at that time, because if there was, you would have.

Forgive yourself, because there is immense power in forgiveness.

Power Process 12

1. Is there anyone in your life you need to forgive, so you can set yourself free?
2. Do you need to forgive yourself so you can set yourself free?
3. In what areas of your life would forgiveness make a positive difference?

Action: What one action could you take today to move you closer to forgiveness?

III.

THE POWER OF FUN

"There is nothing more precious than laughter—it is a strength to laugh and to abandon oneself, to be light."

—Frida Kahlo

As adults, we often compartmentalize fun. We believe that there are right and wrong times to have fun. But when we were children, fun was woven into everything, even when it "shouldn't" have been. At school we may have been passing notes back and forth in the classroom, or at home we might have been giggling into the early hours of the morning when friends were sleeping over, and playing tricks and jokes on each other in stern adult settings.

Then we "grow up," and suddenly we must be very serious. Adults have to work, and work is not fun. Although our working lives are shifting rapidly right now, many people are still tethered to the idea that the week is for work and the weekend is for fun. Or "On vacation I will have fun!" For some people that's only two weeks per year of fun.

But it is a wise person who sprinkles fun into their life when and where they can. It is good for our mental health, our work, our relationships—our whole experience of life is enhanced when we add as much fun as possible.

In 2019 I had the pleasure of interviewing Marie Forleo, the highly successful American entrepreneur and business teacher, for the Australian launch of her debut bestseller *Everything Is Figureoutable.* She has been named by Oprah Winfrey as "a thought leader for the next generation" and, as I found out when I traveled around Australia with Marie, her team, and the Business Chicks (Australia's largest and most influential community for women) team on a five-date tour, she has a lot of fun doing it.

Anyone attending those events would have watched us doing Marie's "jet-lag dance" up onstage and would have joined in too. Dancing there with our shoulders dropped back, arms dangling, groins gyrating, a sexy sneer on our faces, we were experiencing the power of fun.

I was attracted to Marie's YouTube channel *MarieTV* when I started my first business over ten years ago because of how supportive and helpful her content was to me at that time. I loved her quirky sense of humor and the funny videos. She showed her viewers that business could be fun. Years later, the amount of fun we had onstage was in full alignment with what I had admired about her in my early years of business. She values fun. And as a dancer in her earlier life, she has now woven dance into her brand and her business message. Not only does it say, "Enjoy who you are," it is also a reminder that fun is a powerful tool and shouldn't be underestimated as we create our lives.

At a Business Chicks leadership gathering, founder and global CEO Emma Isaacs and I spent days finding ways to put huge amounts of ice down each other's backs at unexpected moments. Why? It was fun. I won that game. We are currently in the middle of a three-year "BOO!" competition. When we are at events together we both plot how to scare each other by jumping out and saying "BOO!" Why? Because it's fun.

Power does not have to be about being serious. Remember, it is "the ability to do something or act in a particular way." Moments of fun, whether spontaneous or consciously created, add to our overall experience of life. Fun gives us a positive outlook, it makes us happier, it fuels our creativity and our connections. As far as I am concerned, we live for a very short period of time and it is the wise person who chooses to insert as much fun as possible along the way.

Many years ago when I was engaged by the Wanderlust brand to coach and facilitate at a New Zealand event, I decided to create a women-only session based purely on fun and play. The first thing I said to the one hundred or so women who attended the session was, "If you are here to look cool, this is not the session for you. It is impossible to look cool and have this kind of fun at the same time."

Then the women had to find a partner as quickly as possible and follow my instructions: "One of you is going to carry, one of you is going to be carried. We are going to have a piggyback race. And we are not going to have a discussion or an apology about weight, or any other conversations about our bodies. If you waste your time having 'that chat,' you will have no chance of winning. And trust me, you want to win because you will want the prize!"

I asked everyone to line up, and told the carriers to get ready to carry and the carried to get ready to mount. There was much chuckling and laughter.

I had a passenger on my back, and with one hundred women chuckling and laughing, I counted down—three, two, one, GO!

We had fifty carriers with fifty passengers who headed toward the finish line as fast as they could. Not all the horse-and-passenger teams made it to the finish line—some fell over, but they had the time of their lives trying to get back up again. And those of us who had finished were egging them on to continue. One team laughed so hysterically that neither of them could get up.

It reminded me of the time we had a three-legged running race when I was an actor with the Royal Shakespeare Company, and I laughed so much I peed my pants. Which made my friend laugh even more.

When the winners of our piggyback race asked what the prize was, I told them, "The first prize is the five minutes of unadulterated fun you just had, and the second prize is the memory you just created."

Corny, but true.

We also ran a three-legged race, where two people have their inside legs tied together and have to walk or run a certain distance tied together. We played "stuck in the mud"—a version of tag where if you are caught, you must stand still with your legs wide apart so that someone can go through your legs to free you. We also did some laughter yoga, a form of yoga that uses laughter to release stress and connect people. This was so hilarious for some women that they cried so hard they couldn't get up, which made them laugh and cry harder, which made everyone else laugh harder. We played, we fell, we laughed, we let go of any stresses or insecurities in that brief hour.

This "childlike" fun, the fun that is not fueled by alcohol, is rare for a lot of adults. Many of the women who played that day told me they hadn't had so much innocent, natural, endorphin-driven fun for years. It made them feel young, vibrant, energized, lighter, and less stressed.

Some of them shared with me that my preamble of "no body-apology conversations" at the start allowed them to get on with it before they had time to tap into their body insecurities and ruin the fun for themselves.

Fun is powerful, but you have to be willing to look silly, to let go of control and risk embarrassment.

And if you're really lucky, you may even get to pee your pants in public.

Fun is powerful.

Power Process 13

1. What is fun for you?
2. When did you last allow yourself to look silly, stupid, or out of control?
3. What is your most memorable moment of fun?

Action: What one action could you take today to inject more childlike fun into your life?

IV.

THE POWER OF PERMISSION

"In my youth I fought for equality. I wanted to participate in the men's game. But in my mature years I've come to realize that the game is a folly."

—Isabel Allende

In most cultures, the power that has been given the most airtime is the *power over* model, and in most parts of the world this power has been perpetuated and maintained by men.

Known by some as "the sausage party" (I have to say I laughed so hard when I first heard this phrase!), these parties are created by men to serve themselves and each other. This form of power has harmed men and women. No one likes to be dominated or shamed into submission, and yet we may have tried to grasp this form of power for ourselves. I treated Ruth from my childhood in the way I did because I was led to believe that there was only one form of power, only one way to have the ability to do something in a particular way. Now I have the wisdom to know that there are many ways to have power that also allow you to sleep soundly at night.

In her poem "Free as a Human," Denice Frohman writes, "I heard a woman becomes herself the first time she speaks without permission."

Many women begin asking for permission from a very early age.

"Can I climb the tree?" asks the girl, and while she is waiting for permission, the boy is already climbing the tree.

"Can I do this project?" asks the woman, while the man is already doing it, making it up as he goes along.

"Can I sit on the board?" the woman says, instead of putting herself forward for the position.

Something I was told very early on in my coaching training was "Masterful coaches have their own coaches." There are many reasons why this resonated for me. Firstly, as a credentialed coach I am required to have a mentor coach who makes sure I am meeting the requirements of my professional association, the International Coaching Federation. As a business owner I would never ask a client to invest in a service that I did not find valuable enough to invest in myself. And finally, I am a human. Just like my clients I benefit from having a safe space to explore my obstacles, honor my strengths, and create a life that honors my values. While working with my coach, Belinda, I remember a session where I asked her if I was at a point in my career where I could fly business class for my speaking engagements.

"Who are you waiting for permission from?" was her response.

I wasn't conscious of it, but I had been waiting for someone "worthier" than me to give me permission to travel in a way that allowed me to do my best work.

In so many situations internal permission is what we need, not permission from some external power. We have to say yes to ourselves before someone else can say yes to us. We will never be able to live and lead in the ways that we desire until we give ourselves permission to do so.

I was facilitating Brené Brown's Dare to Lead™ program for an organization that works on the front lines with marginalized families. It was an honor to work with this organization because it was people like this who looked after me when I transitioned from "unofficial" foster care to state care. It was people like this who gave me the feeling of agency in a situation where I had little to none.

If you are aware of Brené Brown's work you will know that she uses the metaphor of the arena, which comes from Theodore Roosevelt's "Citizenship in a Republic" speech (often known as "The Man in the Arena"). The meaning of this speech is that whenever we are in a vulnerable situation we are "in the arena." The arena represents a place where we are at the mercy of emotional uncertainty and risk, and yet we know the arena is also the home of bravery and courage.

As a Dare to Lead™ facilitator, part of my role is to share my experiences of doing the work as well as facilitating the work. So when I was going through this section with the participants, I shared with them that I was currently extending my bravery and courage.

For the past five years or so, I have chosen to no longer pursue a speaking agent. I adore having direct and real connections with my clients. I decide how much I will charge for my work and who I will work with—there has to be an alignment of values or a shared mission. In the speaking industry, there is a hierarchy of fees for different types of speakers. In the "leadership" category, the highest-paid "noncelebrity" speakers are White men—no surprises there.

I worked for months with Belinda on the topic of my fees to determine whether they represented the value I bring to the audiences I connect with and the stages I speak on. I had a block about increasing my fees. Although I believed in my worth as a speaker, I was not charging accordingly. My inner patriarchal voice kept reminding me to "stay in your place." Belinda kept asking me to "look for the evidence." What were the concrete markers for the value I gave as a speaker and as a client? Then, as an objective voice, she generously shared with me all of the evidence she could see.

It included consistent feedback from speaking clients and audiences that I left participants feeling connected and empowered—connected to their lives and themselves, to the people around them, and to a bigger purpose: the purpose of women collectively supporting each other to thrive. Yet I was seeing speakers who left me feeling cold and disempowered, telling me how to live my life (because what had worked for them must work for me), and at the time they were getting paid triple what I was being paid.

What I came to realize through these coaching sessions was that I was unconsciously waiting for a White man, or at least a White person, to give me permission to charge what I was worth. I was waiting for them to deem me worthy.

From a young age I was raised to believe that as a Black foster child with White parents, I had to be chosen. And if you are "chosen," you do everything you can to *stay* chosen, no matter the cost. I want to explain to you the part-unconscious, part-conscious scenario I had created for myself.

When it came to my speaking career, I realized I was waiting for one of the straight, able-bodied White men to choose me, to grant me permission to join the club of highly respected speakers who charged what they were worth. When I realized this was not going to happen, I thought I would have to expose myself by going up to those White men in suits and asking for permission to join their club. If I was allowed in the club either I would have to take a White man's place (apparently there is little room at the top), and I doubted that situation would be well received, or one of them would have to be my supporter, with my career intertwined with his—and if he left the club, where did that leave me?

So let's look at this scenario: me, a Black woman with a shaved head, sitting in a sea of White men. And as I sit there I know that if I want to stay there, if I want to be chosen, I have to play their game—I have to belong to them, to be one of them. I have to hide parts of myself so that I can be accepted and be welcome in their club. Stay chosen, no matter the cost.

It felt exhausting, and I wasn't sure this club was worth the admission cost—the cost of questioning my worth.

In that moment, I knew I did not want to be a member of their club anymore. I didn't want to ask them for permission, because I knew I would be hustling for my worth to keep my position. I realized two things: one, I would never belong with them, but two, the life-changing realization was that I no longer *wanted* to. I didn't need them to choose me. I could choose myself.

When I let go of wanting to belong, to be chosen, another reality presented itself. A reality where I could build a different club—a club where all the people who did not "belong" had chosen themselves and wanted to be at the top of their game. The difference of feeling I had when seeing this image was profound. When I wanted to be in the "boys' club," I felt nothing but tension and hustle; when I was in the "club of belonging" that I had built with like-minded others, I felt nothing but freedom and belonging.

In the "boys' club," the energy was serious and tense, with those who were afraid of losing their seat perpetuating a feeling of scarcity—if I give you what I have, I lose. In our club we were laughing and talking to each other, building the club together, experiencing abundance—if I give you what I have, we both have more.

As for that hierarchy of White men, some of those men jumped ship. Tired of the hustle, they too wanted freedom and belonging, and we welcomed them with open arms. The others were so busy refusing permission, they completely missed how things were changing rapidly around them.

And that is the reality I choose to move forward with, the vision where those reaching to serve in a larger way are building power for and with each other. It is the future we move toward every time we decide we do not want to hustle for our worth or hide parts of ourselves to belong.

If life is a game, I want to play a different game with a bigger board, with more diverse pieces and players, and an outcome where more people win and the winners create inclusive games for more and more people to win. There is so much more room at the top than we have been led to believe.

When we wait for permission from others, one of the vital steps we miss is the power to give permission to ourselves—to choose ourselves. Are you giving yourself permssion to try? To begin? To put your imperfect hand up?

You can decide "I am ready" instead of waiting for someone else to tell you that you are ready. It is only when we feel ready internally that the external affirmation can be empowering. And together the internal and external validation create a powerful force.

So in the situations where we are chosen (partners, jobs, auditions, awards), these experiences may enhance our experience of ourselves, but the external validation doesn't dictate our experience of ourselves.

Give yourself permission to choose yourself long before anyone chooses you.

There is deep wisdom in choosing yourself.

Power Process 14

1. Who are you waiting to get permission from?
2. How do you hustle to gain this permission?
3. What are the impacts of your hustle?

Action: How can you give yourself permission today?

Power Story

Eranthi

When I was twenty-four and working on a national project in a major telecommunications company, my manager died suddenly of a heart attack and the director approached me to see if I could take on the lead. Suddenly I was overseeing eighteen people across Australia, most of whom were older than me.

My model of leadership over the next seven years, which I quickly adopted from the senior management team, equated to being tough, working long hours, over-functioning, and ignoring my human side. Power was about the control of knowledge and people.

All this changed when I suddenly became pregnant and had my son Aiden. My attention, time, and energy completely shifted to the new little human who was totally and utterly dependent on me, and my working world suddenly felt alien and inhospitable.

So in 2004 I made the decision to leave corporate life and set up one of Melbourne's first day spas, opening a second one shortly after. But I fell into the same trap, working longer and harder, six days a week—and by then I had two little ones under three. Over the nine years I ran this business I became disconnected from the original joy that I had for it—the original creative process—and ended up selling it.

When I set up Aika Wellness, my current business, I was determined to do things differently. In the past, I struggled with asking for help and delegating tasks to others, as I saw this as a sign of weakness. I knew this was something I needed to change to avoid repeating the same mistakes.

Confronting this has been paradoxically the most frightening and liberating feeling. After migrating to Australia as a child in the mid-1980s, I saw how hard my parents worked, starting from scratch to reestablish themselves in our new country. I set an expectation for myself at a very young age that as a migrant and a brown-skinned woman I would have to be totally in control of everything and work doubly as hard as my White peers to be visible and valuable in the workforce. If I didn't over-function both at work and at home, I felt a sense of panic that I would be exposed as a fraudster who had somehow managed to fool people into thinking that I was of value.

Learning to rely on others to manage the operations of my business made me feel incredibly vulnerable, and I still struggle with the need to do it all. I am also learning that my power and worth do not lie in the control I have over a situation, how hard I work, or how others perceive me. I now give myself permission to rest and do whatever brings me joy, working at a pace that feels comfortable for me. Being a leader in this new way has made me feel more connected to my team. Now it feels like we are all part of something greater than each of us.

The greatest gift has been giving myself permission to have a flexible working life. I can finish early so I get to pick up my daughter from school. I can take an afternoon off and have lunch with my son and hear what he is learning about in his psychology class. I often take a morning off to go for a long walk with my dogs and lie on the grass, feeling the sun's warmth on my face. These are my new definitions of success and power.

49 years old. Founder, spa and beauty business

V.

THE POWER OF WORDS

"A woman with a voice is by definition a strong woman. But the search to find that voice can be remarkably difficult."

—Melinda French Gates

When working with clients, I am very present to the words they are using, because our words do create our world and the way we position ourselves in it.

When it comes to setting actions, the client may say, "I will try to . . ."

"I'm pretty sure I will . . ."

"I'll do my best to . . ."

"I might, if . . ."

But there is no commitment in any of these words. They are weasel words—a great way of pretending you're committed when you're not.

The words "I will . . ." create our future actions.

Sometimes a client might describe a situation to me and then finish with, "It's interesting."

Sometimes it is an interesting situation, but I have found that we tend to use the word "interesting" to cover up other thoughts and feelings, such as "disappointed," "scared," or "unsure." A client said her situation was interesting but when I probed further she said, "I feel like I'm losing what's important to me."

As women we have been socialized not to "know," to be

affable and unimposing. We have learned to ask permission before we speak and not to express bold thoughts for fear of not being liked.

While working with a senior leader in technology, I noticed a pattern in her language. After our first few sessions I asked her if she knew what she was talking about.

"What do you mean?" she asked.

I told her that I had observed her saying. "I think . . ." in situations where she had a firm knowledge of that subject or situation.

"I know," she said. "I do it all the time."

"What have been the benefits for you speaking this way?" I asked.

"It's what got me this leadership position," she said. "I have been in this industry long enough to know how a woman has to behave to get to the level where I am."

"What would happen if you did not shy away from your knowledge and expertise?" I asked.

"In the early days, I really don't believe I would have reached the position I currently hold, but now I'm here, I don't need to do that anymore," she said. "I also don't want the women coming up behind me to take on this form of personal diminishment."

We brainstormed other words she could use in her vocabulary.

"I know . . ."

"I believe . . ."

"In my opinion . . ."

"My thoughts include . . ."

Her ability to identify her speech patterns and why she had adopted this way of speaking gave her the power to change how she led, not only for herself but for the leaders following her. Having this realization enhanced her ability to own her power.

When we look at language and power, two words to deliberately add to our vocabulary are "I am . . . ," because the words we use after "I am . . ." are the most powerful words.

When we talk negatively to ourselves we may use "I am . . ." as a way to punish ourselves: *I am stupid, I am not good enough, I am a failure*—if we say these phrases often enough we begin to believe them.

But when we are being compassionate to ourselves, we can use "I am" in a more empowering way: *I am learning, I am doing my best, I am making progress.* If we say these phrases often enough we begin to believe them.

Use your "I am . . ." with caution, because these two words will create your experience of yourself.

To build our lives and leadership without apology, we need to be conscious of our language. As women we apologize a lot of the time. Unless we are focused on our words, it is easy to diminish ourselves to ourselves and in the eyes of others.

When we are actually having a thought, saying "I think . . ." is appropriate. But otherwise, we have other choices:

"I know . . ."—because you do.

"I believe . . ."—if this is your belief, own it.

"In my opinion . . ."—if this is your opinion, own it.

"My thoughts include . . ."—they are valid, so own them.

Words to consciously remove:

"Just . . ."

"It's only me."

I cannot tell you how many times I hear articulate women share a story or a statement of fact that is very clear and understandable and then they end their sentence with "Does that make sense?"

Of course it makes sense. You make sense.

While listening back to a social media clip of a podcast interview I had done, I heard myself saying "Does that make sense?" at the end of a story I shared. What I had said made total sense. I am aware of this minimizing language and still I default to it—the conditioning is strong.

Along with you, I am learning to shift my vocabulary, to speak myself into power instead of out of it.

I make sense—and so do you.

Other ways we can diminish our voices are to change our tone, to make everything a question even when it is the answer—a foolproof strategy for women. We can employ methods of laughing or giggling to minimize the impact of our words. If you are not sure if you do this, observe yourself with people you feel one hundred percent comfortable with. If you don't giggle and laugh when you speak with them, there is a chance you have employed this strategy with others. It is another pattern for women.

Neurodiversity champion and Instagram sensation Dani Donovan is a woman who celebrates her self-esteem and power. I discovered her work a few years ago when someone sent me a great graphic called "E-mail like a boss" that identified the power of the words we use in emails. In her graphic, Dani points out how we can reframe our emails. When you realize your schedule matters too, an email with the sentence "What works best for you?" becomes "Could you do . . . ?" If you're explaining that you know what you're doing, "I think maybe we should . . ." becomes "It'd be best if we . . ." In the same vein, "Could I possibly leave early?" becomes "I will need to leave at . . ." and "Hopefully that makes sense . . ." becomes "Let me know if you have any questions."

I suggest you seek out this powerful woman on Instagram. I completely changed how I wrote my emails after adopting her suggestions. Such small "redirections," such powerful results. Every single one of these redirections puts you in a place of confidence, agency, and power.

Even though these changes seem small, they take practice. When I first shine a light on the way a client uses minimizing words, they may switch their vocabulary straight away or it may take years of practice. We have learned to speak in a particular way because it has served us as a collective—minimizing our voices has allowed us to survive. But in minimizing our words, we minimize ourselves and our potential again and again and again.

We can learn a new way to be in the world, and building a powerful voice is a good place to start.

It's not "just you." It's YOU.

Power Process 15

1. Which of these minimizing habits do you use most?
2. How have they served you?
3. If you could practice dropping just one of these tactics, which would you choose?

Action: What one action can you take today to power up your language?

Power Story

Heang

Working in a global team means that there will generally be a number of people in team meetings who don't understand cultural references and "inside jokes."

As a relatively new member of the team, with much less experience than most of my peers, I struggled to find a connection with anyone in my team onshore. I did, however, find that I was able to build quite a close bond with my peers who were situated offshore, in other locations. I would often have a laugh at my own expense about how I couldn't really understand what was going on in the ivory tower, despite working there.

As time went on, my feeling of disconnectedness to my team and my work grew. Sometimes I didn't quite understand the work and the strategy being discussed, but I was too afraid to ask—for fear of looking stupid or, worse, that my contribution would be overlooked or considered not worthy. I felt that it was both easier and safer to just stay silent. This of course was a vicious circle, with my disengagement leading me to tune out of conversations altogether, missing important information and key work opportunities.

I was feeling isolated and alone. I am ashamed to say it now, but I was wallowing in self-pity, feeling oddly satisfied by blaming everyone else for the situation I was in: the team should engage with me; they should do more to include me; they should check in with me to ensure that I understand things. It was a downward spiral.

Several months into my coaching, I started adopting an action-based approach to my problems. I recognized that I was at the center of the situation—that my thoughts and behaviors were not resourceful and I was not taking any responsibility for my part in it. I also realized if I didn't feel I could contribute or understand the context, there would be others who would be feeling the same, particularly those in other locations whose first language was not English.

It wasn't long until the opportunity for me to use my voice arose. At our next virtual team meeting, the conversation very quickly took a turn down "Acronym Road." I could feel myself starting to get frustrated and tuning out, when I saw the faces of my international colleagues. We were all so used to nodding politely and agreeing with the speaker. But this time I held up my hand and said that I did not understand. I used my voice and expressed my concern that things were not clear to me. I looked at the group again and noticed my other colleagues nodding in agreement. They couldn't understand either!

As a result, the meeting slowed right down and things were clarified until we were all clear on the issue at hand. When the meeting ended, I closed my laptop with a satisfying snap and a smile on my face. I was slightly shaky, but I felt amazing! I now had clarity with my work, and the metaphorical "barrier" I had created around myself was well and truly obliterated.

Over the next few days, I received emails and messages from my international colleagues, thanking me for speaking up. My "little" action of putting up my hand and asking for clarification opened the door just that little bit wider for others to do the same. As a result, we were all clearer on what we needed to do, and in a short time, we started delivering on our team objectives.

As with many of my "Aha" moments during coaching, this one hit me like a brick over the head. I was in my safe little comfort zone for so long, blaming everyone else and denying my part in the situation. By taking back my control and responsibility, I took back my power; and by using my voice, I enabled others to step into their power too.

40 years old. Coach, banking and finance industry

VI.

THE POWER OF INITIATION

Initiation (noun): The action of admitting someone into a secret or obscure society or group, typically with a ritual.
1 The introduction of someone to a particular activity or skill.
2 The action of beginning something.

Initiation involves the task of entering into a space or place, knowing that you will reappear changed. You don't know how, but when you emerge, you will be changed—there is no escaping this fact. Opportunities for rites of passage can be a crisis that falls upon us, like COVID-19, or they can be consciously created.

Puberty, for example, is a developmental process that all humans experience, and many cultures have initiation practices to mark this time. Moving to another country, parenthood, marriage, divorce, sickness, and spiritual awakenings can all be seen as initiations and experiences that transform us along the way.

And then there are rituals. We ritualize certain actions and behaviors to guide the way in our initiations, to make the transformation easier or to bring a sense of reverence. Initiation and ritual go hand in hand. Religious rituals may be some of the first rituals that come to mind, but there are many others. We create rituals to honor initiation and to celebrate our coming out on the other side. Baby showers, weddings, and funerals are some of the most common of our rituals, but they can be as unique and significant to you personally as you want—such as a person shaving their head before starting chemotherapy, or a divorce ritual to end one chapter and begin a new chapter.

We can resist initiation—fight the need for the human spirit to transform and grow, fight the inevitable change. Or if we are wise, we can surrender to the sometimes uncomfortable experience of transformation and growth, knowing that who we are when we come out the other side will serve the next chapter of our lives.

In 2015 my husband and I took our children out of school and traveled around Australia for 387 days in a trailer named "Beauty" and a beast of a four-wheel drive, named "Beast." While in Kakadu, in the Top End of Australia, we had the privilege of being invited to a beautiful river festival where young Aboriginal boys were being initiated into their local dance traditions by the older men of their community. It led to a conversation between my husband and me about initiation and how important this ritual is for teenagers—that if their elders do not create rites of passage for them, they will create rites of passage for themselves that we may not think ideal.

So we have created our own rites of passage for our family. When our son Benjamin turned twelve, he and my husband walked the Larapinta Trail—a 138-mile hike in the Northern Territory. And when our youngest, Ibiyemi, turned twelve, we chose the Bibbulmun Track in Western Australia, at the height of the wildflower season. The track is 600 miles from end to end. We chose to walk the first section, 130 miles over fourteen days, but ended up walking 155 miles due to some wrong turns.

From the very beginning, I wanted Ibi to have ownership over the walk. Part of the initiation experience is stepping out of childhood and moving toward a level of responsibility and independence. Ibi decided the distance we would cover every day. They were already an experienced hiker and camper, and I fully trusted them to know how far they could walk and what the long-distance challenge day would be. Ibi chose the meals and snacks that would fuel them, with minimal consultation from me, and they would carry all supplies and equipment except the tent, which I would carry.

Most days we walked an average of nine miles. The beauty of walking in the bush is the silence, the smells, the air. We saw so much beauty that first day; we had rests as we needed them, and we enjoyed being "free." One of the reasons we adore multiday hikes is that all you do is walk, eat, sleep, repeat. A rhythm forms very quickly. The next few days were similar: flowers, beauty, heat, peace, and snacks.

Being out in the bush with a savvy twelve-year-old did make me reflect on all of the myths about the "scary outdoors" I'd heard growing up in England. I am so glad they have a powerful relationship with the land and nature. One day Ibi said to me, "I am more scared in the city than I am out here." I was in awe of their confidence in the bush.

Although this was to be Ibi's initiation, it was also mine. Mother Earth threw some challenges our way. When we were just over a week into the hike, we had to climb two very steep mountains in breathtakingly fierce wind and rain. We managed to mentally tackle the mountains because we knew we could put dry clothes on at the other end. But when we got to the hut, everything was soaked—jackets, sleeping bags, socks, fleeces. Everything.

It was a miserable afternoon being cold and trying to dry wet clothes in the rain. The huts on the trail are three-sided, with wide wooden platforms (similar to bunk beds, but with no mattresses) for multiple hikers to sleep on. And as we were the only ones at the hut, we decided to put the tent up on one of the platforms for extra warmth and protection from the rain.

As we settled down for the night, thunder heralded a brutal storm. I think it only lasted for about fifteen minutes overhead, but it was terrifying. I lay there holding Ibi tight, singing the lullabies I used to sing when they were younger. I was trying to keep my voice as calm as possible, but it was shaking and I was petrified. Ibi was shaking in my arms and my heart was almost beating out of my chest. I held tighter with every flash of lightning and clash of thunder. When we first arrived we had read a plaque next to some hut ruins. We both knew that the hut we were huddled in was the rebuilt version of one that had been struck by lightning a few years earlier. Our fear was real.

"I want to go home, Mummy," Ibi whimpered.

"I know, darling," was all I could say, because right at that moment, I really wanted to go home too.

I honestly didn't know if we would survive the night. All I kept thinking was, "If we die, at least we are together in each other's arms."

Once the storm had passed, it took us a while to settle down because we were both pumped with adrenaline. I hardly slept that night, just wanting the sun to come up. When I woke up I was so relieved that we were okay, that we were alive. And as I looked at Ibi sleeping, I burst into tears of pure relief.

The following day we had planned to stay in an old worker's cottage at the top of a mountain (the trail hut for this section of the trail). But when we were half settled in, the skies darkened and I feared another storm. I decided to check if my phone had reception and it was confirmed: there was another storm coming. I let Ibi know, and decide what to do next.

"Mum, I don't want to be up here all alone on the top of a mountain with a storm coming," they said.

We had already walked more than ten miles that day, and to get to the next hut we needed to walk another nine. So nearly twenty miles altogether, two days of walking in one.

Ibi wanted to know what I wanted to do, but I said it was their initiation walk and they had to choose.

After a moment, Ibi said, "Let's do it!"

It was 3 p.m., so we had roughly three and a half hours of daylight left. It was hard, but we kept moving forward. The rain came. The dark came, and Ibi stayed up front with the headlamp. Ibi led and I followed. Eventually we reached the hut. We were exhausted, but we beat the storm. By the time it came, we were settled in the hut and had other hikers for company.

The next day was our last day. There was no fanfare when we finished. As we walked through the town, no one knew what we had just accomplished—that we had just walked 155 miles in thirteen days, mother and child leading each other. No one knew that we had been challenged by the elements and by our own minds. No one knew how far we had both come, both internally and externally.

But we knew.

I asked Ibi for one word to sum up the initiation walk.

"Pride, Mum. I'm really proud of myself."

There is power in getting through the tough times, through the struggle and the unknown.

Initiation is not always as intentional as our initiation walk was, but if you look back at your life you will find you have been initiated along the way.

My husband and I created these initiation experiences for our children to help them to navigate their teenage years with a real and grounded experience of who they are, what they are capable of, and how resourceful they can be.

As adults, it is important that we put ourselves in conscious initiation, that we too have real and grounded experiences that reveal who we are, what we are capable of, and how resourceful we can be.

We have many choices for initiation as adults—from taking yourself out into the bush alone for a period of time, setting yourself a physical challenge, moving to another country, writing that novel, building a house, getting rid of half of your possessions, or embarking on a pilgrimage. It is impossible to undertake any of these activities, if they are new to you, and not be a different person on the other side.

There is power to be found in knowing who we are, what we are made of, and the many initiations and transitions we have had along the way. We become wiser with each misstep, with each challenge met and each success gained. We are not born with wisdom—we build it through our lived experiences and our bravery.

We have the ability to initiate ourselves into our own wisdom.

Power Process 16

1. What initiation experiences have you had in your life?
2. What did you learn about your yourself?
3. How have these initiations shaped you?

Action: What action can you take today to credit your life journey so far?

VII.

THE POWER OF BOUNDARIES

Boundaries—clarifying them, setting them, and maintaining them—is a topic I am often asked to speak on.

Although there are different ways to describe what boundaries are and how they work, I prefer to explain them like this: Boundaries are intentionally crafted limits and guidelines that we put in place to respect ourselves and other people. Boundaries allow us to wear our dignity on our sleeve.

If we want to give our best at work and at home, we need to manage our energy and our time so that we can deliver sustainably, and this is where boundaries become our best friends.

I am a boundaried person—I have learned to be. I have boundaries not because I'm unkind: I have boundaries because I want to be the kindest person I can be. I don't want to walk around feeling resentful, overwhelmed, and exhausted. I've never met anyone who is kind when they are resentful, overwhelmed, and exhausted.

Every woman I have ever met who has put strong and respectful boundaries in place has done so because the cost of not having boundaries became too great. Chronic fatigue, burnout, disconnection from her own needs, and a sense of disconnection from others led her to put those boundaries in place. It is only when we understand our value, our worth, and our physical, emotional, and mental capacity that we create boundaries.

One reason we can struggle to set boundaries is the idea that we are the providers and supporters of everyone else's needs, which hardly gives us the time to be the supporters of our own needs. I have written in my previous two books about the curse of the "good girl," and I believe that one of the reasons women struggle to set boundaries is that it flies in the face of what we are told we should be as good girls (or good women, when we grow up). Good girls do not say no.

To mess around with societal and gender expectations can feel risky, because if I'm not available all the time, what is my worth to others? Do I have worth if I'm not needed?

These can be confronting questions, but they are necessary.

If you are one of the few women who has given yourself the time to work out what you truly want from yourself and your life, what you want to contribute and how you want to contribute it, you understand that setting boundaries is the only way you can fulfill your own life plans.

But there is no point in having boundaries if you are not clear on what is important to you. Setting boundaries is not about saying no at random intervals for no reason, like it's some sort of power game. Boundaries allow us to protect what is important to us, including ourselves. So before setting boundaries, spend some time thinking about what is most important to you—what do you most need to protect?

In my own life, I have decided that my spiritual practices and physical fitness are very important to me. I have boundaries in place in terms of my work so that I can attend to my spiritual practices and fitness. I have created boundaries so that I have time to practice yoga, meditate, journal, work out, shower, have a good breakfast (for me a good breakfast is an unrushed breakfast), and spend time getting ready for my clients that day.

Well-being is important to me, so although I could possibly achieve all these things in a particular time frame, I give myself more time than I need so that I don't have to rush. By the time my workday begins I am truly ready for my clients. I am physically, mentally, and energetically ready to be a calm and present coach for them.

You may be reading this thinking, *Well, it's okay for you.* But to be able to choose to work this way has been a long time coming—ten years in the making. It all began with one of the most potent coaching exercises I have ever done. I was asked to write down my perfect day. And my perfect day included having ample time in the morning to look after my mind, body, and spirit.

When I was home with young children, I would work on my business, as many parents do, after the children were in bed. Before I had children, when I was an employee, I did what I was paid to do, including the work hours dictated to me. This is sometimes the trade-off for a regular income. Working for someone else has pros and cons, and working for yourself has pros and cons. Working for yourself (if you have set up your business this way) offers you flexibility and freedom, but not necessarily a regular and predictable income. Working for someone else gives you a regular and predictable income, but not necessarily flexibility and freedom. At one stage of my life being an employee worked for me; now being a business owner does.

If you are an employee, depending on your unique situation and what is important to you, the boundaries you put in place may look different from those of a business owner. As someone who works with both business owners and employees, I know that both groups struggle equally to set and maintain boundaries, because as I said earlier, women can struggle to make our own needs as important as everybody else's needs.

I have had to work out who I am and how I want to live, and then I have had to do the confronting internal work and the challenging external work, putting boundaries in place so that I now have choices I never thought I could have or create. I do not take my situation for granted—in fact, I choose to see it as a responsibility. I get to choose how I work, so my work needs to be useful and impactful for others.

Also I am very aware that as I change and grow, so will my boundaries. What works for me now will change, and when it changes, I'll create new boundaries to support me and what I choose as important at that time in my life.

Boundaries are the gift that keeps on giving. But setting and communicating boundaries can be challenging—you may have to be a little uncomfortable along the way. I learned very early on that the uncomfortable feelings that may come with setting boundaries are nothing compared to the freedom that results.

Boundaries are not a one-size-fits-all solution. Depending on your unique situation, stage in life, responsibilities, and resources, the boundaries you need to put in place will vary. But when working with clients or facilitating boundaries in groups, I have a three-step process that I use to support boundary setting:

1. **Clarify** what is important to you. What do you need to protect? Clarify the boundary that needs to be put in place.

2. **Communicate.** Who does this boundary need to be communicated to? Communicate it clearly.

3. **Commit.** It is your job to commit to and maintain your boundaries. If you have wishy-washy boundaries, it's on you, not the other person.

Just like presence, setting boundaries is a lifelong practice. In different life stages, different aspects of our lives need protecting. And we will make mistakes along the way.

Just the other month I had a situation where I was caught off guard and agreed to do something I don't normally do in regard to how I conduct business. As I was caught off guard, I didn't take the time to respond; I reacted and said yes. My default reaction was to be "good," but as soon as I put the phone down, I felt resentful, not good.

Although I had already said yes, I did manage to say, "Can you please put that in an email so I can have a look over your request?"

Because I had already said yes to the request, I did want to deliver on it, and luckily when I had it written in email form in front of me, I was able to see a way that I could fulfill my "Yes" that didn't then encroach too much on my boundaries.

But I did resent fulfilling my "Yes," and it was a good reminder of why I have strong boundaries in the first place. The Kemi who carried out the request was not the kindest Kemi I can be.

We are not always going to be able to maintain boundaries every time, but unless we have them in the first place, we are open and available to everyone all the time.

If you consider yourself a people pleaser, I have some confronting news for you—people pleasers rarely please anyone . . . least of all themselves.

It is impossible to have the capacity to please everyone around you. What ends up happening is that either you are not able to fulfill all of your "Yeses," so you feel bad and the people you say yes to are let down. Or you are spread so thin that what you do deliver is nothing you are proud of, in work or in life. We cannot be everything to everybody; in fact, we can't be everything to *anybody*.

Build your boundaries and protect what is important to you. The confronting truth is, no one else is responsible for your feelings of resentment, overwhelm, and exhaustion. These feelings are a direct result of you not having clearly communicated boundaries.

Are you willing to be uncomfortable for a moment so that you can be kind, energized, and free in all the other moments?

Boundaries create power.

Power Process 17

1. What three areas of life matter most to you?
2. How do you protect and honor these areas of your life?
3. What one boundary could you put in place for each of these areas?

Action: What boundary do you need to communicate to someone today?

Power Story

Louise

One Friday morning, I walked into my office, exhausted. I sat down on the couch, took a deep breath, and just cried my heart out. I could not understand why I was feeling this way, why I was so exhausted, emotional, and frustrated. I sat in silence for about thirty minutes and then it suddenly dawned on me that I was a slave to my own business that I had created nine years earlier with my husband. A business we created to have freedom, flexibility, and choice, none of which existed.

My days would start at 4 a.m. and I was working six to seven days per week, fourteen to sixteen hours per day. I missed out on many birthdays and other celebrations. I had no time or energy to catch up with friends and family. My relationship with my husband was nonexistent because we treated each other like business partners. I started to hate the business we had created—a business that was actually flourishing, super successful, and that employed twelve people. I knew something had to change immediately, because if it did not change then everything I had ever worked for would fall apart overnight.

The first area I focused on was changing my leadership style—an area that was failing me. I had employees who were supposed to take the workload off me but instead were creating more work. I realized I was always trying to be the "nice" leader and making sure everyone on the team was happy. I would avoid communicating clearly to the team because I did not want to offend them.

But this style of leadership proved wrong—I was constantly being taken advantage of and having to put up with poor performance, gossip, and staff turnover. I no longer wanted to be that nice leader—I wanted to be a clear and kind leader.

I worked on putting in systems and processes that would first of all work for me and my husband, and then everyone else. We worked on implementing boundaries with clients and employees and communicating very clearly what was acceptable and not acceptable. This sounded simple, but I was terrified of setting boundaries because I was afraid of what everyone would think of me. It took a lot of confidence and encouragement to make it easier. Kemi and I would often role-play the harder conversations, which built my confidence for when I had to have those conversations with the team and clients.

Looking back, I wish I had known about setting boundaries from the very beginning, because my boundaries now allow me to plan and execute my day with a lot more peace and calmness.

And as for those sixteen-hour days, my hours have reduced significantly. I have Fridays and weekends off and my relationship with my husband is stronger than ever. I can confidently say that I am no longer a "nice" leader but a clear and kind leader, and I am respected more than ever by the people who work for me.

What a game changer this has been in my life. By taking a leap of faith, acting upon it, changing my leadership style, and setting clear boundaries, I now have more freedom, choice, and flexibility than ever before.

34 years old. Founder, recruitment industry

In summary

Wisdom comes in many forms.

To forgive is wise. It releases us from suffering and it can release others too.

To have fun is wise. We are here for but a very short time, so we want to make the most of it.

Granting ourselves permission to use our voices is wise—so that we can live as a full expression of ourselves and give others permission to do the same.

Honoring ourselves through our words is wise. By doing this, we create our world with our words and we can create powerful worlds for other women.

Initiation gives us wisdom. It demands growth, and as living beings, we need to grow.

Creating and maintaining boundaries is wise. Not everything or everyone is important—protect what is important to you.

Wisdom not only comes with age and experience. It is also formed in moments, in our actions, and in our choices. Wisdom brings with it power.

When we betray our wisdom, we diminish our potential and our power, and we risk betraying ourselves. Some of us have been doing that for far too long already.

It's time to listen to and act upon your wisdom.

Part 5

EQUALITY

"You are powerful and your voice matters. You're going to walk into many rooms in your life and career where you may be the only one who looks like you or who has had the experiences you've had. But you remember that when you are in those rooms, you are not alone. We are all in that room with you applauding you on. Cheering your voice. So you use that voice and be strong."

Kamala Harris

I.

E IS FOR EQUALITY

We all have a role to play in shaping global equality, in seeking it for those who have less than we do. We also have a role to play in owning the equality that sits within each of us, no exceptions.

Equality. Where to start? I honestly do not believe that you would be reading this book if you did not have an interest in social justice and global fairness.

How to dig into the complexities of global hunger, gender inequality, racial inequality, climate change inequality, class system inequality? There is so much; the topic of global equality is fraught with difficulty.

And yet dig in we must. We must dig in, in our own individual ways—we must do what we can to make a difference. We can choose to see this as a duty, as a burden, or as an opportunity. As far as I am concerned, what is important is that you do see, and when you see, that you don't look away; that you are willing to be uncomfortable to make others comfortable; that you are willing to take action when and where you can, in the very small ways and the very big ways.

The stories that outline this Power Principle are stories of inequality and hope. They are stories of separateness and togetherness, of what is happening now and of what is possible in the future. We dive into the complex topics of race, worthiness, and diversity, through story and lived experience. The Power Stories shared by Cortina, Kylie, and Annie highlight how inequality and equality show up in our lives and how they inform who we are and who we want to be.

The world will not right itself until people are willing to see each other, sit together, and, when needed, stand up for each other as equals.

II.

THE POWER OF RACE

In 2017 I went to the United States with my husband, Emrys, to take part in the notorious New York Marathon.

We stayed in Brooklyn the week before the race with one of my oldest friends, the incredible fashion photographer Tatijana Shoan, and her family. Tatijana and I became an unlikely duo in drama school and formed a tight bond. We didn't click at first, but sometimes the strongest friendships begin with friction.

For a few days before the marathon, Emrys and I went walking around Brooklyn and New York at our leisure, without a care in the world. One of the joys of this city, and the reason I fell in love with it the first time I visited Tatijana in 1996, is the number of people there who look like me. It is such a diverse place. I loved riding the subway because there seemed to be at least seventeen different ethnicities in one car. I felt like I belonged.

I am an avid theater lover. So when we were in New York for the marathon, I naturally wanted to go to Broadway, and we were lucky enough to catch a couple of shows. One night we decided to try our luck and see what show we could get tickets for. When we arrived at the theater, Emrys went to the ticket counter and I held back to find something in my bag. But when I joined my husband at the counter, the ticket seller glared at me and snapped, "What do you want?"

Then, nice as pie, he said to my husband, "Excuse me, sir, I am so sorry about this."

I was the "this."

The ticket seller was White. My husband is White. It seemed, in this man's mind, that there was no way the nice White gentleman and the Black person could be together, and it was obvious he felt it was his job to save the White person from the Black person.

Emrys and I have been together long enough for him to have learned about, seen, and understood the microaggressions of racism. I never need to explain my lived experience to him or justify my reactions—he witnesses them. The reality is that many mixed-race marriages do not make it because of the stress and complication of racism.

In a very firm tone, Emrys said, "This is my wife," and pulled me close to him.

The ticket seller simply looked at him and said, "I am so sorry, sir, my mistake."

No apology to me. He didn't even acknowledge me.

And that is the power of race. A judgment can be made about a person in a split second.

As a Black person, I have to choose in every moment whether to defend myself against every racist slight. My challenge is to hold on to my sense of self through every slight and every choice.

I was able to hold on to my sense of self in the ticket-counter incident because my husband pulled me toward him and advocated not just for me, but for us. But my husband is not always there—nor should he have to be, and nor would I want him to be.

Near my home in Melbourne, I once walked into an upscale liquor store to have the owner jump out from behind the counter to ask me what I was after. This was not an act of service: this was an act of fear.

Instead of turning around and walking out, I held firm. I told him I was looking for a white wine to go with a coconut curry I was making. He then proceeded to walk me to the back of the store.

"These wines are on sale," he said. "You should find what you're looking for here."

Then he walked away and stood where he could watch my every move.

I had not said that I wanted wine that was on sale.

I stood there staring at the sale wines with my hands clasped tight in fists and trying to hold back tears. I was frozen to the spot trying to work out what to do next. And what I did next was reductively childish.

In that moment the only way I could hold on to myself and "prove" myself to him was to take a bottle of Veuve Clicquot champagne from the fridge and walk to the counter. *I'll show him I can afford more than discounted wine!* And then I hustled for my worth with a complete stranger.

I made sure that I spoke very well and dropped in a few middle-class-isms so that he would know that I was not a danger to him, that I was just like him. I asked him about his elderly father who was stocking shelves. I asked how long the store had been in the family. I asked him all the questions a nonthreatening Black person might ask. I hustled. And it worked.

I know it worked because after I'd talked about my children he reached behind the counter to give me an ornate box in the shape of a music box—promotional packaging from a wineglass brand—for my children.

I thanked him for the box, smiled, and walked outside. As I walked away I felt a little less worthy than when I had entered the store to find some white wine to go with my coconut curry.

I never gave my children the music box. It had cost me too much; so much more than the champagne.

I have spent so much of my life proving that I am worthy to complete strangers, and I know I am not the only person of color who has had to navigate the world this way.

One beautiful sunny day in Melbourne I was in the car, windows open, my two young children in the back seat, when I caught the eye of the driver in a car coming the other way. I didn't like what my instinct told me: something about the energy he gave off and the way he looked at me made me uneasy.

As his car got closer, I just managed to close the window as he shouted, "You fucking nigger!"

Thankfully my children didn't hear his words and could live without knowing them for a little while longer. But for people who look like me, hearing those words and being exposed to this kind of racism is a constant reality.

Sticks and stone may break my bones. But names can break me too.

So does silence.

Recently in a supermarket line, as I was unpacking my items from my basket, I was very taken by the conversation the cashier was having with the customer ahead of me. They didn't know each other but had connected instantly and were enjoying their conversation, laughing a lot. It was really nice to watch.

Then it was my turn, and in a good mood after watching this conversation I said warmly, "Good morning!"

The cashier looked down and didn't reply. I thought maybe she hadn't heard me.

"Hi," I said.

She mumbled a quiet "Hi," but didn't meet my gaze.

I felt my stomach drop. That's what happens to me: my gut drops away.

I knew what was going on. So did my body.

I was caught off guard.

I was not prepared.

I was deciding whether I was going to defend, attack, withdraw. Cry, run away, or confront the woman.

I suddenly felt incredibly small in front of this stranger who refused to acknowledge me. I was no longer in a good mood.

I paid for my groceries silently and walked away, battling the urge to turn around and see how the cashier was responding to the next customer, who was White.

My thought process was, "Maybe I got it wrong. Maybe it was not racism at all, maybe I misread the situation. Maybe she suddenly developed a migraine. Maybe."

Sometimes the need to answer the "Am I worthy?" question takes over. I had no intention of doing anything about the situation—such as confronting her, for instance—but my sense of self needed to know if I was wrong. I wanted so badly to be wrong.

I turned around.

And there she was, chatting away happily with the next customer, laughing, and smiling.

I gained no pleasure in being right.

I carried my shopping to the car and sat there staring into the distance as the tears fell.

Sometimes I am consumed with anger in the face of the constant microaggressions. Sometimes I just flick them off. Sometimes I feel so fragile, the weight of it feels too much to bear.

And yet, I bear it. We Black and Brown women bear it. Because if we get angry about it, well . . . we know how that goes.

That is the power of racism. It has the power to keep you small. No matter the work you do. No matter your contribution to society. No matter how much money you have in the bank. No matter if you are a good neighbor and community member. No matter how many awards you have. No matter how much you give to charity. No matter your title. No matter.

Power Process 18

Women of color in a White majority

1. What are the ways you "hustle for your worth"?
2. When was the last time you experienced racism, and how did you handle it?
3. Did you tell anyone or did you push it down?

Action: What one action can you take today to own your worth?

White women

1. Do you have an ethnically and culturally diverse network of friends and colleagues that exposes you to the lived experiences of others?
2. When was the last time you pushed racism aside because it felt too hard?
3. What do you need to learn or unlearn about racism and how you benefit from race privilege?

Action: What one action can you take today to educate yourself?

III.

THE POWER OF WORTH

Starting and running your own business is one of the most challenging and rewarding personal development journeys you can go on.

Setting out on your own in business is not just an expression of your passion or commitment to contributing to society and the economy in some way, it is also a statement of your perceived worth. What do you believe your qualifications, experience, training, and skills are worth? What do you believe your services or products are worth to other people?

For female business owners, this can be challenging, because we have to declare our worth in the marketplace. We have to be willing to say, "I honor myself and the value I bring." Many women fall into the trap of letting other people decide their worth and value, because they want to be "liked" and don't want to upset anyone. Been there, done that.

But as we grow alongside our businesses, if we don't honor our work, and if we don't value our worth, the business we began from a place of passion will become our undoing. If we can't honor our worth, no one else will.

Many years ago I was invited to work with an organization I had admired from afar for a very long time. I had been asked to speak at a variety of their events, but although my work aligned with the vision of the brand, it turned out the way they worked did not align with me. One of the first red flags for me was their lack of communication once I said yes to working with them. For a while, I had a weekly routine with my assistant. Every Friday I asked the question: “What has been your highlight and what has been your challenge this week?” The name of this organization was the challenge for many months.

I have a clause in my contracts involving payment of a fifty percent up-front deposit to secure me for a speaking engagement. After too many emails back and forth, my assistant eventually secured the deposit with the organization, but it was like pulling teeth. I had agreed to do multiple events for them, which meant I was tied to them for longer than the usual speaking opportunity.

I adored working with most of the team, and the audiences constantly reminded me of why I love speaking and facilitating. They were openhearted, fun, and ready for growth. But my contact was a challenging personality to work with, and that started to cloud the positives.

The balance on my deposit was due two weeks before the first event, and seven days out I still had not received payment. After numerous emails from my assistant to the finance team, and finally one that included the organizer, there was still no balance deposited into my account and no communication about when it would be paid.

I had been working with this organization for over a year at this point, and it was no longer exciting or fun for me. I decided the next event was going to be my last with them.

For my last event, my client had paired with a second organization—one I had deep respect for—and I had been asked to emcee a special event for them, which I was happy to do. I had been waiting on information for over two weeks so that I could fulfill my role for the second organization, but I hadn’t received it. I didn’t like the thought of letting down the second organization, and without the information I’d been promised, I wouldn’t have enough time to practice the script.

Everything came to a head one morning when I realized how disrespected and powerless I felt. It had been a painful process up until this point, and any joy I'd had about doing the job was gone.

I remember calling my husband in tears of frustration to talk through what my next steps could be. Not only is my husband a good sounding board, he is also a lawyer, which does have benefits in situations like these. I asked him if I could break the contract because I hadn't been paid. My husband assured me that the organization was in breach and I could dissolve the contract.

I was about to send an email explaining this but decided to call my coach, Belinda (it also helps to have a coach on your side), and the brief conversation I had with her changed something in me. I came away ready to call the client myself and not hide behind an email.

This was an organization much bigger than me, and I felt at the time that causing trouble for them could negatively impact my career. Plus, the person I was dealing with was a very confident White man. It was a big deal for me to think that I could meet his power, that I could ask for what I was owed.

With shaking hands, I called him.

There were many elements to that call. First he tried to diminish my concerns and made fun of my request to be paid according to our agreement. I reminded him we had both signed the contract, and since I was willing to fulfill my end, he needed to fulfill his.

He then went into full *power over* mode. He tried to belittle me by telling me about all of the "big names" he had worked with, and that I was not one of those big names, "darling."

Then came the misogyny: "All you have to do is throw on a frock and say a few words."

I told him it was insulting that he believed that was all I would be doing. So then he tried manipulation, telling me that the business had cash flow issues and he had to put food on the table for his children.

This was a hard one but I took a breath and responded with, "So do I. We all have to put food on the table."

He then tried emotional blackmail, to which I responded that we should keep focused on the business at hand.

I remember he paused at that moment. He was thrown.

That's when I said, "If the balance is not in my account within the next forty-eight hours, I will not be speaking at the event."

There was silence.

Then he said, "Not a problem, Kemi. I'll make sure the money is paid to you within the next four hours."

I thanked him for his time.

The balance was paid within two hours and he sent me an email to confirm it.

I was so emotionally exhausted from that conversation, I had to take a nap afterward. But the experience changed how I do business, how I honor my worth in a monetary sense as well as my self-worth. Honoring both is how I own my power. I am proud of myself for having robust business terms and agreements that honor my value and allow me to power up from a base of equality and worth.

Life is full of difficult conversations, and the hardest ones are those where we feel we have less power. Often, if we dare to go into the conversation, we go in on the back foot feeling as though we are "causing trouble," even when we are in the right. I had to step up to have that conversation. I had to speak, even though it scared me. I asked for the support I needed to have the conversation—from my husband and my coach. I couldn't go in alone, because my socialization told me it was a bad idea. I can honestly say it was one of the hardest conversations I have ever had to have when it comes to my business and owning my worth, and it was the conversation that elevated my understanding of the importance of owning my worth without apology. It was a conversation that changed my business forever, and for that I am thankful to that client—the situation forced me to step up.

We sometimes believe that a successful difficult conversation happens when our hearts are not pounding, and we are not shaking, sweating, or trembling. But these are the signs that the conversation matters to you—and after you've had it, nap if you need to.

When two people go into a conversation, they both have the right to be there and to be heard on equal terms. If each person can leave the conversation with no less worth than when the conversation began, that is a new level of conversation.

And the world needs a new level of conversation.

Power Process 19

1. Are there certain people in your life who cause you to question your worth?
2. What is the impact on you?
3. What would you need to do to shift this dynamic?

Action: What one action can you take today to own your worth?

Power Story

Cortina

I lay on the operating table after giving birth to healthy twin girls and felt the blood rapidly leaving my body—all due to an oversight by my obstetrician that shouldn't have occurred. I remember feeling simultaneously hyperalert (I could die) and incredulous (I'd been told he was "the best"). I was hemorrhaging and the surgeons were working furiously to save my life. Ultimately, I ended up losing more than two quarts of blood.

But the challenges didn't stop there. The following months were some of the most painful of my life. My resilience was put to the test. There were further complications—more oversights and mistakes.

For me it was a wake-up call. These weren't simply errors. I'd flagged a number of concerns, but they'd been ignored and dismissed by my doctor. I knew I had to speak out. I faced the fear that rose up—of not being believed, of no one caring, of being perceived as a difficult woman. I wrote an open letter about my experience that was shared with the CEO and the board of directors of the hospital. Changes in the hospital procedures, training, and accountability resulted.

But the most powerful outcome of writing that letter is that I became conscious of where I'd been ignoring and dismissing my own needs. My experience, while traumatic, was the catalyst for me appreciating and valuing my own worth.

For a decade I'd been playing a self-appointed role as the queen of "yes to everyone but me." Silencing my feelings. Ignoring tension in my body. Taking on more than I should, striving to be likable, and equating my worth to how much I was able to accomplish, while sleeping as few hours as possible. I'd effectively become a type A cliché. All these "yeses" had landed me in a place where I was paddling furiously, to and fro, without a clue as to where I was even going. Busy. Tense. Unfulfilled.

I'd left a high-paying corporate job that I hated to follow my dream of running my own company. Taking that step felt euphoric and liberating, but old habits were reemerging. Instead of staying true to my vision, I was making compromises, saying "Yes" when I felt "No." As more people became involved, the company was evolving into something I no longer recognized as my own. There was a voice inside me that seemed to be saying "STOP," but everything was hurtling along at such a rapid pace that I didn't know how to get things back on track.

Fast-forward to me lying on that operating table. After the events that occurred, I was effectively bedridden. Unable to walk more than a few feet, with a baby in each arm and a toddler at my knees, amid a global COVID-19 lockdown. I had no choice but to be still. And with stillness came clarity.

I needed to get clear about what I really wanted and to let go of habits that were holding me back.

I started to journal. I became exquisitely aware of self-limiting beliefs I held—some my own, some transplants from others. Beliefs at the root of all those unwanted "yeses"—the belief that other opinions were more valid than my own; that I wasn't smart enough; that to express feelings was a form of weakness.

I expanded. I became even more focused and intentional. I created personal principles—words that repre-

sented my most authentic and truest self, my values, my hopes and dreams, and my worth. These principles became my compass.

At first it felt almost radical to say no when an opportunity or offer arose that didn't quite align with my personal principles. But gradually, as I became more attuned to my inner voice and my worth, it no longer felt radical: it felt like the only rational choice. In the end, I chose to step away from my company. It was the completion of a lesson in letting go of an unproductive pattern of behavior, to trust my own intuition and value my worth.

40 years old. CEO and founder, women's health industry

IV.

THE POWER OF EQUAL

It was my great pleasure to be invited to Necker Island—Richard Branson's private island in the Caribbean—in 2018. I have admired Richard Branson since the early Virgin Music days, when I was a teenager and didn't really know what an entrepreneur was—I'd liked his commitment to fun and frolic.

I accepted the invitation to attend a women's leadership immersion, not to meet Richard Branson. (Apparently you never know how long he will be there, because, well, he has quite a few projects on the go!) I was going to spend time with other businesswomen and take time out of my business to reflect on it and to listen to world-class speakers such as Elizabeth Lesser, author and cofounder of the Omega Institute for Holistic Studies, and Cady Coleman, an astronaut.

On the speedboat from the island of Tortola to Necker there was champagne and sunshine. It was going to be a great few days in the tropics.

On the first night at the welcome dinner, I sat next to Jean Oelwang, the CEO and president of Virgin Unite, which is a not-for-profit entrepreneurial foundation. Jean and I clicked immediately on topics ranging from endurance running, our plant-based lifestyles, and the mysteries and mayhem of marriage. Jean is an exceptional leader, and after such a rich conversation, my cup was so full I could have flown back home that night completely satisfied.

The next morning, after completing my yoga practice with a view over the Caribbean Sea, I showered and headed off for breakfast. Now, I imagined Richard Branson would make a big entrance, perhaps on a chariot with flames, driven by pink unicorns. After all, he is one of the most influential entrepreneurs on the planet. What I didn't expect was to be greeted by him as I was helping myself to some pineapple from the breakfast buffet.

"Good morning!" he said. Not a pink unicorn in sight.

I thanked him for having us on his island, and then asked him a question on behalf of my father-in-law. "Do you have any spare vinyl records left over from the Virgin Music days?"

He laughed and said, "We don't actually have a record player here, but we probably should."

He then asked me where in England I was from, and we chatted casually about British stuff while collecting our breakfasts.

I excused myself, because one introvert knows when small talk is over with another introvert. I joined the other women on the program at a beautiful long table overlooking the ocean, feeling lucky that I'd had a few moments with Richard Branson, and happy about how easily we had chatted. Then he came upstairs, made his way over to the table, and sat next to me.

Over breakfast, the conversation turned to Hurricane Maria, which had swept through the British Virgin Islands the previous year. Richard knew everything about the wildlife that had been lost—he knew how many flamingos had died, how many lemurs had perished. He knew that the flamingos were still traumatized and were not yet laying again; he hoped they would soon.

There was a moment when I realized that my inner voice was saying, "You are talking to Richard Branson about flamingos."

Luckily for him, it turned out there was someone at breakfast who had just spent time in Madagascar studying the lemur populations, so I left them to it and bowed out of the conversation.

I tell this story to show that there is power in knowing that you are equal to everyone you meet. I do not own an island and have no desire to do so. I also do not want the responsibility of 800 million companies, but I do want to stand equal and side by side with anyone I have the fortune to meet. I believe that Richard Branson feels the same. He has no desire to *power over* people; he is more interested in being with people.

When I facilitate for The Hunger Project—whose mission is to create a world where every woman, man, and child leads a healthy, fulfilling life of self-reliance and dignity—I stand side by side with village leaders in Uganda and I know that I am no better than they are. Yes, I have more external resources than they do, but when it comes to our human worth, we are equal.

When I was a child, one of my foster mothers would comment that "Homeless people have brought it on themselves." To her, they were drunken addicts who were dangerous and we were made to cross the street when we came across such a person.

Later, when I was twelve and my sister was nine, we were made homeless. Our foster mother at the time was evicted and she disappeared on us, and we had no fixed address for roughly six months. We were lucky that the parents of our school friends were willing to take us in until we went into the "official" foster care system.

We had not "brought it on ourselves," and I don't believe that any homeless person brings it on themselves. I know that life can kick us in the guts at any moment, and depending on where we were born, to whom we were born, our ethnic background, our sexuality, our gender expression, our physical abilities, and our internal and external resources, we will find ourselves in a place where our equality to other human beings is questioned, either within ourselves or in the eyes of others.

It takes something to own our equality in the face of such

challenges, and yet we are equal because of our challenges. I'm not pretending that I've always known this—in fact, I would say that for most of my life I have not felt equal. For the majority of my life I have felt less and I have been made to feel less. It has taken nearly thirty years of committed personal development in many shapes and forms (including a weekend of naked tantra!) to arrive at this place.

I am equal to Richard Branson. I am no more, no less. I am equal to the leaders in Uganda. I am no more, no less. I am equal to the homeless person. I am no more, no less.

There is power in owning our own equality. There is also power in holding others as equals. Valuing equality empowers everyone.

As a coach, I am witness to and hold space for all forms of human experience, and especially the female flavor of that experience. All of my clients are equal in their humanity. They may not have the same resources or life experience, but their equality as human beings is never in question.

We all have exactly the same range of human emotion. We suffer, we strive, we win, we lose, we have love, we lose love.

There is power in knowing you are equal to every other human on the planet. And if anyone intends to make you feel less equal than them, don't question your equality: question why they need to make you question your equality. It's not about you.

When you know you are equal, you do not have to prove that you are equal. You do not need to hustle for your worth.

We must be able to walk into any space and know that we are equal to every single person in that room.

You are equal. We are all equal. Sit with that for a moment.

Power Process 20

1. How would your life be different if you walked around knowing you are equal?
2. What would you start doing?
3. What would you stop doing?

Action: What action can you take today to establish your equality or someone else's?

V.

THE POWER OF DIVERSITY

"It's not just that I'm a woman of color running for office. It's the way that I ran. It's the way that my identity formed my methods."

—Alexandria Ocasio-Cortez

Many years ago I was very excited to be invited to one of my first women's leadership conferences. It was happening in Noosa, a beautiful coastal town on the east coast of Australia. There were just under two hundred women invited, and it was an incredible event. I met women there who are still trusted friends and colleagues to this day.

On the second to last day, there was a panel discussion on diversity. As we were all gathering for the session, there was a holding slide on the projector screen. It was a patchwork of women's faces, about a hundred of them all pieced together, smiling brightly and confidently.

I looked up at this holding slide and thought, "Where are the women who look like me?" All of the women on the slide were White and yet this was a panel about diversity. I was one of three women of color at the conference, and I can't remember if I was already standing at the back of the room, or if I was moved to stand because I was feeling so uncomfortable.

As I listened to the very esteemed panel talk about diversity on boards, I kept staring at the screen—at the smiling, confident, White faces looking back at me. The panel was focusing on gender diversity, but I felt it was impossible for me to be in that room and not flag what I saw as a misstep. Actually, a complete oversight. Where were the women of color? Why were they not also smiling confidently at us from the slide? Where was the intersectionality in this conversation?

A sensation that I couldn't control began rising up in me. I wanted it to stop because it was uncomfortable. But I couldn't stop it, because there was something more at stake here. My intense discomfort was a sign I couldn't ignore. My internal voice was saying, "You need to point this out. If you don't speak up, who will?"

I looked around the room several times to see if anyone else was about to stand up or raise their hand to point this out. I tried to read the body language of the two other women of color in the room but I could not gauge if they were thinking and feeling the same as me.

My inner voice was saying, "You have to speak up."

But then another chimed in, "You have been invited here. Do not upset anyone."

And another: "Do not be the angry Black woman."

I wasn't angry, but I was definitely getting hotter, and waves of nausea kept sweeping through me. It felt like I'd been feeling intensely sick and uncomfortable for about an hour, but it was only a few minutes.

Before I knew it my hand was in the air and I was invited to ask my question.

I'm sure it was obvious that my voice was trembling as I said, "When I look at the screen all I see is White women. Where are the women who do not come from an Anglo background?"

It felt like five hours had gone by, according to my trembling internal clock, before a panelist responded with, "First we will tackle gender, then we will tackle other forms of diversity. We can't do everything at once."

She hadn't liked my question, but that didn't stop me.

"If I do not see myself or anyone who looks remotely like me on that holding slide, I do not believe you are advocating for me—I don't see that I belong on a board," I said.

Her next response was very dismissive—I certainly felt dismissed—but then something interesting happened. It wasn't only me who disagreed with the panelist; there was a noticeable drop in energy and a few audible sighs of displeasure.

Then there was silence. And then the next panelist responded in a very different way.

"I had not even thought of it like that," she said. "And in future, when I am having the conversation about gender diversity on boards, I also need to take in cultural and ethnic diversity as well. Thank you for bringing this to my attention."

It was so affirming for someone to say they hadn't thought of this, it was a humility that transcended ego or defensiveness. The second panelist was not responsible for the images on that slide, but she knew she was complicit in the system that promoted who belonged where.

I made my way back to my seat. I needed to sit down. I felt very exposed and incredibly vulnerable, and my heart was beating out of my chest.

As soon as my bottom hit the seat, the woman next to me looked at me and said, "Thank you so much for speaking for me. As a Chinese woman I was thinking the same thing, but I was too scared to speak."

There are many differences between African and Chinese ethnicities, but as a minority, she did not feel welcome on boards either.

As we headed off for a break, I was approached by a White man (a sponsor) who said, "It is so good that you said that. I was thinking that too."

"Really?" I said. "I'm curious, do you have an experience of diversity that makes you aware of this?"

"No," he said. "But looking at that picture, it was obvious who was missing."

I liked him.

During the break, many of the other delegates thanked me for speaking up and said how it had opened their eyes to where they were complicit. I must have been inundated because I missed out on the scones and jam that were being served for morning tea—which, for an English person, was a little upsetting.

After the break, the next speaker shared that she has a daughter with a disability, and finding employment for her was very difficult. That's when I realized where I was wearing my diversity blinders, where I was complicit. As I had said to the diversity panel, women of color go to banks, we brush our teeth, we buy cars and yet we are never represented in the media as doing so.

This speaker was saying the same about people with disabilities.

We all have our diversity blinders. Admitting we have them is where we give each other the power to learn and stand together.

Power Process 21

1. Where do you have your diversity blinders on? Who do you not see, and why?
2. What or who has shaped this way of seeing the world?
3. What are the "benefits" of your diversity blinders?

Action: What one action can you take today to own your blinders and increase your awareness?

Power Story

Kylie

In 2019, I participated in a self-development program that helped me realize I was ready to leave my long-standing job and start my own company helping women and leaders transform at a deeper level.

Although I was overjoyed to establish my own business and direct my energy into an area I was passionate about, it was also a time of great frustration. I found getting started was not as easy as I had imagined and it was difficult for me to latch on to one of the hundreds of ideas my inspired mind generated. I attributed my irritation to COVID-19 lockdown, fear, and not being surrounded by the familiar chaos and work pressure I was used to.

Six months into my new venture, I caught up with a friend for a coffee and, while talking about my recent struggles, she suggested it might be worth me looking into a condition that she has—attention deficit hyperactivity disorder, commonly referred to as ADHD.

Interested to learn more about it, I did some research and came across a podcast specifically for women with ADHD. There were many identifiable stories and characteristics that related to my own way of being, especially having long-standing feelings of anxiety and working doubly hard to get things done. As a result, I booked myself in to see a specialist GP, hoping an appointment might help me uncover more.

For weeks leading up to the consult I felt a restless anticipation, stirred by the notion that I might get an answer to some of my lifelong challenges. I wrestled with thoughts of enthusiasm and caution, conscious not to get too ahead of myself.

On the day of my appointment, I felt an unusual sense of composure; the discontent I had been experiencing had lessened. The doctor's diagnosis that I did in fact have ADHD was the affirmation that I was both hoping for and secretly expecting to receive. For my entire life, I had always felt like a square peg trying to fit into a round hole, struggling to comprehend why things came easier to others and fraught with guilt and shame for seeing, feeling, and comprehending things differently.

Walking back to the car I noticed that I felt a great sense of relief and elation, until "Killer Kylie," the self-proclaimed nickname for my destructive inner critic, turned up. "What about the label? What if people think you are dumb? What if no one takes you seriously? What if you stop getting work?"

Having done quite a bit of work on my unhelpful alter ego, I was perceptive enough to stop her in her tracks. Instead of heading down the rabbit hole of doom, gloom, and despair, I used this moment of cognizance to think about my newfound diagnosis in a more constructive way, applying a reframing method I had learned via my coaching studies.

I thought to myself, "What if that doesn't happen? What if this is something that I can use to help others? What if this is about me being able to highlight my strengths, my ability to make the complex simple, to think outside the box, to innovate, to invent, to motivate and inspire others, and to use my natural gifts of curiosity, optimism, sensitivity, and intuition?"

I professed out loud that I would accept my differently wired brain for what it was and use it to my advantage.

While this was a defining and empowering moment for me, acknowledging my ADHD isn't always easy. It is still a condition that is often misunderstood and misrepresented, and I have had to manage my own personal biases and limiting beliefs, constantly reminding myself that it is not an excuse but a reason for how I think and function. Each time I reveal my ADHD, it takes a willingness to be vulnerable and a commitment to being brave.

50 years old. Executive leadership coach, facilitator, and speaker

VI.

THE POWER OF MY BLACKNESS

The Black Lives Matter movement began in 2013. George Floyd's murder in June 2020 was the catalyst for Black Lives Matter garnering global attention, but it is important that I also acknowledge that in both the country I live in, Australia, and the country I was born in, England, Black people are still being murdered because of systemic racism.

Two weeks after George Floyd's murder, I still had not found the words. I found this odd, because I have been a victim of racism all my life, and suddenly I had nothing to say.

I found myself numbly walking around, sleeping a lot, and sobbing a lot.

Then I read a post on social media by a Black psychologist. There were many global conversations about the importance of Black people looking after their mental health and well-being during this time. That was what I needed to read, because I felt pressure to say something but I had no words. Finally, I realized that what I had was my subjective experience and I wanted to share that. I wanted to share my own story and the impact racism has had on me.

I knew that social media was not a place where I wanted to share such vulnerable words. But I have a deep trust and respect for my "Weekly Words" community, whom I have been writing to via email every Friday morning at 8 a.m. for the last eight years. I wanted to share my words with them first.

When the words came, there were not many, just the ones I needed to say. The words I found follow.

I Am Black

I have few words to describe what is going on in the world right now.

I do not watch the news, so I have seen no images. I don't need to and I am not a fan of murder or brutality porn.

As a Black woman who was born in England in 1974, I was a minority by birth.

I was raised by five sets of White foster parents.

I chose to move to Australia, where I am a minority by choice.

I married a White man and I have children who are bi-racial.

The weight you may be feeling now, I have felt for at least forty-two of my forty-seven years.

Those of us who live as minorities were not shocked by the death of George Floyd, nor by the death of Tanya Day here in Australia.

When you live it, you are not shocked.

I am emotionally exhausted and heartbroken.

If you are a person of color reading this, I know that you have had to hide, soften, or polish your story, or have been made to question your lived experiences of racism to make others comfortable. I know because I have had to do this.

If you are a mother to Black sons, I know that you have had to have the conversation with them about their safety in the world. I know because I have had to do that.

You may hold me in high regard because of the work I do or who you know me to be, and yet when I walk into certain places, I am not held in the same regard. When I walk down the street, I am not held in the same regard.

I learned how to hustle for my worth from the age of five.

I am writing my third book [this book], and that is where I am choosing to share my voice about my experiences of race, gender, and power.

I invite you to reach out to your Black and Brown friends. Check if they are okay. Most of us are not.

If they want to talk, listen. That is all you need to do. Ask if there is anything they need right now. And listen.

It is not their job to make you feel comfortable.

It is not their job to answer your questions.

A few things not to say:

I understand. *You don't.*

I can imagine. *You can't.*

I can't believe this is still happening. *It is.*

We live in the same world, but we walk in very different shoes.

The responses I received after hitting "Publish" were touching, humble, and profound. Some were a little awkward, but all were from a deep place of wanting things to be different.

I was asked by many people if they could share my words with others in their life who they struggled to have difficult conversations with about race. Of course, I said yes. Once I had found the words, I wanted them to be useful in any way possible.

And then something happened that I never expected . . .

The morning after I posted "I Am Black," to my surprise, my husband handed me a handwritten letter. He has written me many beautiful letters during our time together, but nothing like this one.

I am sharing this letter with you with my husband's permission because I believe this is part of what "doing the work" is—ownership, openness, and humility.

We have been together for twenty years and married for sixteen of those, and during that time he has had a view into how I experience the world as a Black woman, and as a father to biracial children. We have many conversations about race.

He was a barrister in the case of Yorta Yorta woman Tanya Day's death in custody in Victoria in 2017, so he has a view from inside the system as well as inside our home.

This is the letter from my husband.

My dear Kemi,

I am, always have been, and always will be, White.

People see me and immediately know that I can be trusted, believed, adored; that I am worthy of attention; that I am one of the club, the family; that they can be candid, can tell the old-school jokes; that I can keep secrets; that I am one who belongs to the real order automatically; that I sailed the seas, and conquered, and slaved, and earned my place, with them, at the top; that I deserve, genetically, or by God-given right, to belong with them in the middle, at the top, in the right suburbs, at the right schools, in parliament, and the courts, and the clubs; that I am suitable, appropriate, necessary; that I belong anywhere; that I can do everything or anything, or not, as I choose; that I am right, able, authoritative.

And all of that from one glance, one impression, just of how I look.

What a valuable gift! A magic charm which gives me so much, just when people see me for a moment, a glance.

How easy it is to believe that I am entitled to that gift, like Sméagol (Gollum) who, over long, dark years with only his own conscience to guide him, came to believe that the Ring had been given to him as a birthday present, when in truth he murdered its rightful owner, his friend Déagol, and took it in blood.

I have heard since birth a soft and soothing lullaby—you are so right and good; you deserve everything that comes your way; the world is your oyster, and the pearls inside are yours. Can you imagine how nice it is to hear that song, to see what the world has to offer, and to know that I am entitled to it, that I deserve it, to see what people are prepared to give me, what society is prepared to afford me, just because of who I am?

And so, like Prince Siddhartha, I wandered the world and saw that all was right and good . . . until, one day, I saw behind the set, I heard through the lullaby, that great discordant cry of grief, which was at first so ugly and uncomfortable to my ears—the song of the cost of my gift.

Because the gift of Whiteness is not given, it is not deserved, and it is not free. Like Sméagol, I have learned, and taught myself to believe, that my place in the world was a gift, which I deserved.

But then I heard the song of truth, which sings that the princely power of Whiteness was not a gift, is not a gift, but something that was taken, and continues to be taken, in blood; that was and is taken without consent. That Whiteness is the spoil of an ongoing crime that comprises all other crimes, and dwarfs them in its magnitude; a crime that is worse because it is sanctioned by the law, by parliaments, and courts, and banks, and stock exchanges, and cathedrals, and media; all these sing the lullaby with a deafening, blanketing volume.

But not loudly, or unceasingly, enough to prevent a pure note from penetrating through. I heard that other song at night in Tennant Creek, so far from parliaments, banks, and skyscrapers, as I lay in our trailer, looked up at the ancient stars, and listened to the keening cries of grief, of loss, of trauma, cries of rage at what was taken, in blood and rape, when my great-great-grandparents were already building lives further east and south on the plunder and spoils.

I have never heard that song more truly, it has never seemed more urgent or true, than when you have sung it to me.

I cannot give back what has been given to me because of my Whiteness, because that has already been taken.

But I promise you this: I will do whatever I can to not be silent while the lullaby continues; I will do what I can to raise and amplify the voices singing the song of truth; and in my own awkward way (awkward because I have been raised on the lullaby, and it is the only song I really know), I will try to sing the wrong notes, to squawk or shout, to disharmonize, to try to create dissonance, anything but unison or silence, in the hope that I, and others, can tune in to the lullaby, and realize it is a song, not the truth, and then, I hope, listen for those other songs which tell us, "This was taken, not given; this is wrong, not right."

And I promise you also that within our marriage, and within our home, I will always listen to you if you tell me that I am singing the lullaby, and that I will believe you, because you can hear it for what it is, in a way I will never be able to do.

All my love,
Emrys

I have known my husband for two decades. I "know" him, but I had never witnessed his expression of his privilege in this way. It moved many other White people too, who contacted me to let me know that Emrys had put into words what they had struggled to own and express.

We walk alongside each other on the same path, although wearing different shoes. But one of the things that binds us is the ability to hear each other's lived truth.

Power Story

Annie

For most of my adult life, I've been drawn to matters of racial equity. This was really sparked when I moved from Kenya to Australia as an international student over twenty years ago. What I didn't anticipate in moving to a new country was the feeling of being different and not seeing much of myself reflected by way of representation in the public domain.

Having grown up in a country where most people looked the same as me, to now living in a country where I hardly saw people who looked like me, took a long time to get used to. Taking public transportation, going grocery shopping, and in most of my classes in college, I was the only Black person. I felt just how much I stood out, and many times there was a feeling of being "less than." Not because I thought of myself as less than anyone else, but it was a feeling, a knowing that I was being viewed differently by those who didn't look like me. It's how the conversations ensued—it seemed there was always an inquiry as to how a Black African like me could speak such good English or could afford to study abroad, like perhaps I was one of the lucky ones who "got out."

In the process of really trying to find out where this imbalance came from, why there was such a misrepresentation of Black people who came from Africa, I was drawn deeply into matters of racial equity. I found myself researching why the inequities exist and what can be done to live in a more just world.

As this work pulled me in, I came face-to-face with the

issue of worthiness in different forms: worthiness as a Black woman and worthiness as a contributor stepping into the diversity, equity, and inclusion space.

As I dug deeper to try and understand why feelings of "less than" kept showing up for me, I realized one thing: the power of narratives—who was telling them and how they were being told. I discovered that many of the stories shared about Black people are synonymous with struggle. That ours is seen as a life of poverty, illness, and a lack of proper education. It is that same lack that is tied to the "less than" feeling that kept showing up.

If I was ever to fully own my story and proudly stand on my own feet, I needed to address my issues of worthiness. I needed to find my power. This would involve pulling back the layers I had put up as a way of self-preservation; often being silent when I saw certain things happening that were unjust. It was always easier to be silent. But with time, the silence was not serving me and I knew I needed to step up my courage. Coaching allowed me to dig deeper into the "why" behind the self-preservation. Why did I choose silence as my way of survival?

I was able to pull back the layers, which took me back to my childhood years in school where I experienced bullying. It was during those formative years that my sense of self was shaped. A self that felt it wasn't worthy, because some kids had said so.

I started journaling my feelings, putting pen to paper, and began to undo the limiting beliefs that continued to show up, even as an adult. It took prayer and affirming who I knew I was, and rejecting what others had imposed upon me to really begin owning my story. To hold my head up high and feel deserving and worthy. To really occupy space and allow myself to be seen and to shine, without the guilt of feeling like I need to dim my light so others can feel comfortable.

I've learned that I don't have to look or sound a certain way to earn respect. I don't have to be the most educated or well-spoken to contribute to an issue that I'm passionate about. I am more than enough just the way I am.

I've learned that the power to effect change really comes from within and from doing the inner work. I've learned to own myself and my story, every bit of it, from my appearance to my intellect to my heart. I'm here on purpose and for a purpose. I have a life to live, work to do, and lives to affect. My contribution is needed and I'm here to give it my all.

41 years old. DEI coach and consultant

In summary

Equality, racism, worth, and diversity inform so many of the challenges faced by society. They are challenges we must each face as individuals. There is no doubt the world is changing, and yet we still have a long way to go.

How can you contribute to the change?

It is easy to feel overwhelmed by the enormity of the task ahead, and overwhelm is a sign you are taking on too much, but overwhelm is not helpful if it is an excuse not to do anything at all.

There is no doubt that fighting for the equality of others, and standing in the equality of yourself, will be uncomfortable, challenging, and confronting.

Relationships will change, some for the better and some will come to the end of the road. Power lives in the quest for equality—a power to effect change.

Sometimes standing for equality means you do not laugh at your friend's racist, homophobic, or transphobic jokes. Sometimes it means advocating for your own worth or the worthiness of another, with a pounding heart and trembling knees. Sometimes it means leaving a relationship or a job because you are worth more. Sometimes it is in allowing yourself to be fully seen and to shine brightly so others can see themselves.

At the start of this Power Principle I mentioned that we get to choose how we view our role in creating equality: that we can see it as a duty, as a burden, or as an opportunity. But not everyone gets this choice—the birth lottery is real, so for those of us with privilege, whatever form our privilege may take, we have a choice.

Sometimes advocating for equality on the basis of race, worth, or diversity means giving up comfort.

What are you choosing: comfort or equality?

Part 6

RESPONSIBILITY

"In the long run, we shape our lives, and we shape ourselves. The process never ends until we die. And the choices we make are ultimately our own responsibility."

Eleanor Roosevelt

1.

R IS FOR RESPONSIBILITY

When we take full responsibility for our power, we have the freedom to decide how we use it. We all have the ability to do something or act in a particular way.

Most of us have responsibilities in our lives, but that is very different from being responsible for our lives.

There are aspects of life that we have absolutely no control over. The time we are born, our ethnicity, our physical abilities, our gender, our sexuality, or the family or community, place, or circumstances we are born into.

Every single one of us is emotionally wounded, and every single one of us has emotionally wounded another in some way. Sometimes the wounds we inflict are deliberate, sometimes we aren't conscious of them. Sometimes the wounds we cause are played out in our minds and scripted to make sure the hurt is felt; sometimes we wound others by just being who we are.

Are you taking responsibility for your wounds and your wounding?

Two quotes that deeply resonate for me on the topic of personal responsibility are: "Hurt people hurt people" and "You probably were not responsible for your wounding, but you are responsible for your healing."

I was a ball of trauma and hurt when I powered over Ruth.

When we stop blaming others for what has happened to us, we can focus on what needs to happen for our healing to take place. And let me say this: we will only heal when we are ready. It can be psychologically dangerous to begin a path of healing we are not ready for, which can cause more trauma and wounding. Healing takes time, self-compassion, and nonjudgmental support.

How do we know if we are ready? We can ask ourselves these questions:

- Am I ready to heal now?
- Where do I need to start?
- Who can support me?

I experienced a range of levels of care from five foster families—some provided abundant love and care while in other instances I experienced sexual, physical, and emotional abuse and neglect. I know that taking responsibility is not an easy path. It may be painful, confusing, and confronting, but if we are willing and able to do the work, it will be one of life's rewards.

No one else is responsible for your life, your happiness, or your fulfillment—annoying, I know, but true nonetheless. What I know is that taking responsibility brings me a form of freedom I don't have when I'm blaming others or wishing things were different, instead of making things different.

I want to be free. I love freedom. You?

In this final Power Principle we explore the different ways in which we can take responsibility in our lives—from understanding our personal values and how they form a foundation for responsibility, to our relationship with money, to embodying responsible leadership, embracing privilege, and taking meaningful action. In this Power Principle, there is only one Power Story left to share—the story of Caroline. It encapsulates one of the hardest things to heal for many women: sexual abuse, and its continuing impact.

II.

THE POWER OF VALUES

Values (noun): Principles or standards of behavior; one's judgment of what is important in life.

In my first-ever coach training session, we looked at values and how we could do "values work" with clients. From that first moment I was drawn to this particular aspect of a coach's repertoire. Since then I have researched, experimented, and become very passionate about the power of values.

Over the years, I have crafted my own way of working with clients to support them to understand, choose, and honor their values. One of the many reasons I was drawn to the Dare to Lead™ training was the importance that was placed on values in the work.

Understanding what we value means we have a compass to allow us to be truly content and fulfilled, and when we are content and fulfilled, we have more to give to others. Values assist us in navigating any situation, decision, or action we need or want to take in life. When we find ourselves overwhelmed, angry, frustrated, resentful, lost, confused, or lethargic about what is happening in our lives, tapping into our values refocuses us.

I'm not saying that our values will make sure life is smooth and we will never experience loss, setbacks, or failures—sometimes honoring our values creates loss, perceived setbacks, and failures. What I am saying is that if we use our values as a way of navigating life, we will experience personal alignment and integrity.

Integrity (noun): The state of being whole and undivided.

I had the pleasure of interviewing multi–*New York Times* bestseller and world-renowned coach Martha Beck about her book *The Way of Integrity*. Martha explains the meaning of integrity using its Latin origin "integer," which simply means "intact." To have integrity is to be one thing, whole and undivided.

When we know what we value, we are whole and we experience integrity. We can put our heads on our pillows at night and think to ourselves, *The choices I made today are aligned with who I want to be and what is important to me.*

As a coach, working with individuals on their values is a joy. It is a process of uncovering, in many cases, because often we tend to get caught up in what we think the "right" values are and what we want others to think about us.

So the uncovering includes picking apart preconceived judgments such as:

> Money = bad. If you value money, you're a bad, greedy person.
>
> Peace = good. If you value peace, you're a good person.
>
> Success = bad. If you value success, you're a power-hungry person.
>
> Love = good. If you value love, you're a good person.
>
> Pleasure = bad. If you value pleasure, you're a selfish person.

Then there are those things we call values that are actually rules we impose on ourselves. For example, someone says they value organization but what they actually mean is, "I should be more organized." That is not a value, that is a self-imposed rule.

Our values are not about "fixing" parts of ourselves we think are broken. When we choose values based on what or who we think we "should" be, we can actually hinder ourselves from finding our values. I always joke that no one is allowed to select "world peace" or "love" as their values—we can just assume that we all want world peace and love. With that in mind, how do we identify our values?

Identifying our values isn't as easy as we might think. It's common for people to feel that they know what their values are, only to change their minds when they sit with the idea for a while and realize their values and their actions do not line up. And what we value shifts and changes as we gain more life experience, as we strive for different possibilities and outcomes. Our values change as we change. We are living our own unique lives, and what we choose to value is entirely up to us as individuals.

Although you can go and find values lists all over the internet, in my experience values work is best done with a coach, because you take the time to explore all the options, and have someone to question your choices and invite you to go deeper. Of course, I understand that coaching is not accessible for everyone, so let me share with you a clarifying question that has served me and my clients well when it comes to homing in on our values.

Ask yourself: *If I could only navigate the world with three values, what would they be?*

I have had the same three core values for many years now: connection, growth, and well-being. These values have guided me every day, in every way. If I am stuck when making a decision—whether to work with an organization, how to parent my children, and so much more—these are my filters, my questions.

What would connection do now? How does this affect my connection to myself and others? What would growth do now?

How does this decision facilitate my growth or the growth of others? What would well-being do now? How does this action support my well-being, or support the well-being of others? These questions always give me the answers I need, and I trust the answers.

You will see that the second question on each of these values is aimed at others, but this does not have to be the case. It works for me because of my chosen values, but if I had a different set of values, the second question could be my downfall.

If you are reading this book there is a good chance that you also value growth. It may not be a core value, but you appreciate personal development and its pathways to living and leading authentically.

What we must be careful of is not using our values as a way to dictate how someone else "should" live their life. Because I value growth, it doesn't mean that I require the people I spend time with to value growth. I do not use my values to filter or measure other people. My values work is for me and me alone. They can be used as a filter for how I treat others; but not to control or change others—except for my husband (I'm a work in progress!).

Using values as questions allows us to see them live in the world.

One of my clients identified well-being as one of her values. When we dug further, her actions showed that despite her values, she prioritized her phone. Her constant connection to her phone took time away from her doing the things that enhanced her well-being. Her first action, once discovering this, was to turn her phone off at a certain time each night so that she could focus on getting enough sleep and nurturing her relationships at home.

Values should not be aspirational. Aspirational values are an oxymoron—either you are living your values or you're not.

We have to take personal responsibility for knowing our values, and actioning our values in our lives.

Power Process 22

1. Can you name your three core values?
2. If not, can you carve out the time to do some values work, either alone or with guidance?
3. If your values are clear, how can they support you and any challenges you are currently facing?

Action: How can you live into your values today?

Power Story

Caroline

I am a survivor of childhood sexual abuse. The language in this statement is, in itself, where I take back my power, where I own my truth and know that though this truth is not affected by my choices, it is a part of my story. Today, I am a woman who stands proudly as a survivor, no longer a victim, no longer weakened or crippled by the shame and hurt created by my abuser.

This shift from victim to survivor did not come naturally. I have been a work in progress and continue to be a work in progress, taking it one day at a time. A huge shift for me was understanding my values and how I had confused the concept of values and morphed them into rules, to restrict me from harming myself and the people around me. Rules to protect me from getting close to others and being hurt.

When your values are designed to protect and restrict you, there is a freedom that is lost. I had convinced myself that my values were the best way I could be in the world, the only way I could be safe.

When I chose my values to be gratitude, accountability, and having a positive impact, I thought that I was giving myself a belief system, but instead I was giving myself a set of rules to live by.

I told myself to be grateful, don't complain; I'd already been through so much, I needed to look at all that I had today, and I needed to be grateful for all of those things. I reminded myself not to ever take anything for granted, because I knew that life could be so much worse than this. There was a deep inner voice that told me to keep being the good girl, to not be greedy, and to remember that I already had more than enough.

I chose "accountability" because I believed it was important to always take responsibility for my actions, to always be in control and not to let anything step outside of the tight walls I needed to build around myself. No one had taken accountability for my abuse, so I would ensure that accountability was something that everyone needed to have if they wanted to be a part of my life, even if this meant inflicting my values and rules on the people around me.

The harshest rule of all was "positive impact." I had a strong determination to be safe and to do no harm to others, but I always sensed the vulnerability that came when things were too good to be true, when I let people get close to me or became close to others.

I had created behavior to deflect and numb myself, and this caused me to often destroy the good things in my life, the calm moments and the feelings of joy, before they were taken away from me. My behavior had been destructive in the past, I had hurt many people and pushed away people whom I loved, hiding behind armor and walls. I feared that this pattern would continue, so I imposed this value, the strictest rule of all. I told myself that all of my actions were to have a positive impact, that there was no excuse for destruction for the sake of it. I convinced myself that there could only be good done, so I could continue to be the good girl.

Through coaching, I moved away from my values being strict rules to my values being the beliefs that guide the manner in which I treat myself and the world around me.

My true values are purpose, integrity, and gratitude.

I have shown up day after day as a leader for myself as I move away from the walls surrounding me as a victim to the freedom of being a survivor. Today I live a life of purpose, making clear decisions on how I live my life and the legacy I will leave. I am grateful that I chose to be a survivor.

39 years old. Entrepreneur, lifestyle management

III.

THE POWER OF MONEY

Like many people, I have had a complicated relationship with money. The very idea that we even have a relationship with money was initially new to me—as it may be to you—yet examining that relationship has changed everything for me.

In my experience, being raised by six different sets of parents in six different homes gave me six "lived" ways to experience money. This is what I learned: money is a way of life; it is important but it is not everything; money is bad; there is never enough money; those who have it got it in unethical ways; money is energy; people who have money or want more money are greedy; money is to be taken even if it does not belong to you; money comes and goes; you can take money from others through deceit and manipulation; money can bring you freedom; money should not be spoken about; if you do speak about money, it must be in hushed tones; money is a powerful tool for blackmail and emotional abuse; money can be used as an extension of your values; money is dirty.

I learned to be ashamed to think about money, to earn it, to talk about it. I learned that we have to work very hard for money and we will never have enough of it. I learned that money can be a force for good, that where we choose to spend our money can have an impact on our communities, political systems, and global economy.

It was confusing to have witnessed and experienced money in so many ways, but through all this the one thing I knew for sure was that money has power.

I began my first foray into entrepreneurial endeavors when I was roughly eight years old, sewing and knitting little craft items and selling them to my friends at school. At eleven I started my first newspaper route. I liked getting up early, whizzing around on a bike, feeling purposeful—but even better, I liked earning my own money.

Then, at the age of thirteen (I looked older than my age), I worked illegally collecting empty glasses in a small village pub that was masquerading as a wine bar. I did not earn much money, but it gave me freedom to get out of a foster home that contained various forms of abuse. At the same time, I started babysitting for Jenny, the woman across the street. Jenny had five children, and I would babysit for five hours a night, four or five days a week. I would receive one pound per hour. It was a lot of money to me. I felt rich and powerful in a situation where I was powerless.

With that power I bought myself and my younger sister a taste of freedom from our neglectful and abusive foster home. With my earnings we could escape every weekend to the local shopping center and movie theater.

My final foster parents, Sue and Russell, were middle-class. Sue and Russell were frugal and respectful of the money they had. They tithed some of their income to their local church. They did not celebrate money or flaunt it in any way. In fact, they lived like they had a much lower income than they received as a non-governmental organization worker and a high school teacher. They lived below their means—a very admirable and responsible way to live, but at that time I thought they were just plain boring. They had more money than I had ever experienced, and I couldn't understand why they just didn't spend it all (not thinking about how, from the moment I arrived, I increased their expenditure tenfold!). Overnight, my life had been upgraded emotionally and financially.

When I left school, I went to baking school and one of my first entrepreneurial successes was selling the goods I made to my neighbors. Twice a week I would walk up and down our hilly street in Hertfordshire, in the southeast of England, and sell my iced buns, loaves of bread, and other sweet and savory treats. To be able to create something people wanted, and be financially rewarded for it, was so empowering.

I was able to go to drama school for five years because Sue and Russell paid for it. As soon as I left drama school at eighteen, I became a working actor. My first job was on TV playing a lead role in a soap opera, and I was paid a very large sum of money on a weekly basis. In my first year as an actor, I was earning more than Sue and Russell's salaries put together.

My foster grandmother Christine (Sue's mum) was the only grandmother I had ever had a close relationship with, and when she passed away, I received a generous inheritance from her. I was deeply moved that she included me in her will. It changed my life, because she stipulated that the money could only be used for a home deposit—she wanted me to have my own home, a home no one could move me from. At twenty-two, with my earnings as an actor and with the inheritance, I purchased my first home.

I worked successfully as an actor for about seven years until I realized it was not my calling. The money I made through acting was not worth being unhappy for: unhappiness and lack of fulfillment cost a lot in the end, and my salary was not covering those costs. One of the hardest and best decisions I have ever made was to leave a lucrative and fun acting career to work as a chef in a resort in Thailand for a man I had met once in a pub, for no money, only food and board.

When I look back, I realize that having many primary caregivers over my childhood meant that I had a detached relationship with money. Families came and went; money came and went.

Over the years I have come to know many truths, and one of

the most important is that the ultimate responsibility for women is to have agency over our money—to understand it, to ask questions about it, and not to give ownership of it to others by default. This does not mean that you need to have buckets of money. It is about understanding the money you have and your relationship with it, and how money works in the relationships you have.

A few years into my business, Kemi's Raw Kitchen, I knew I wanted to grow it to be successful. I knew that would mean I would have to start being more responsible for the money coming into and going out of my business. I shifted from an accountant I had found near my local stores to one who came highly recommended by a friend when I told him I wanted to manage my business finances better.

The financial investment was much more than I had been paying for my previous accountant, but I realized that if I was going to "step up" in this area of my life, I had to be responsible for the gaps in my knowledge about managing money.

I remember my fear going into that first appointment. I had promised myself that I would not pretend to understand what was being said by the accountant if I didn't understand what was being said.

At the outset of the meeting I said, "I did not learn anything about how to manage money growing up. I didn't grow up with money and I don't understand money. I am now earning a good income and I want to know how to look after it. I will not pretend I know what you are talking about if I don't know what you are talking about, and I will constantly ask you questions so that I do understand."

The response from the lead accountant was great: "I wish more people would be honest about their lack of money knowledge. It means that we will know how to best look after you. Ask as many questions as you like."

I left that appointment so proud of myself. I am glad that I was vulnerable enough to speak the truth and have now been with those accountants for over ten years. It was a life-changing meeting.

I have worked with various coaches from the moment I started my business—a coach to start the business, a speaking coach, a coach to learn how to create online programs, and more. But none of these really touched on money, so I decided to take on a business coach to support me with managing the money within my business. I listened to money podcasts hosted by women, read books, and learned how to work on my money mindset—which is continuous work. I still listen to podcasts and read books about money because now I enjoy learning about it. I even have a "Money Matters" playlist for when I am doing my balance sheet and forecasting. I have a bookkeeper and accountant so I don't necessarily need to do this, but I enjoy the ritual, and the power of knowing.

Within a marriage or any long-term relationship, money holds power, whether it brings you together or acts as a barrier.

My husband and I have had a difficult journey as far as our relationship with money goes. We found out that we were pregnant after only nine months of knowing each other. Emrys was a law student and I was a working woman with my own home and an abundant lifestyle. At twenty-eight I moved to Australia with Emrys, six months pregnant, to start the next chapter of my life—motherhood. We lived with his parents, I was no longer working, and he was working full-time. Now he was earning the money, and when I began asking him for money, we fell into the classic gendered situation. He was "holding the purse strings" and paying the bills, while I was at home and basically receiving an allowance. I also fell into the gender trap of thinking that because he was a man, he knew better than me about money.

I am still surprised to think that as soon as I became a mother, I gave up the power and agency I had as an independent woman.

My relationship with money in my marriage was an emotional roller coaster. I could hardly have a conversation about money with my husband without feeling inferior, crying, and leaving the room. One of the reasons this happened repeatedly was that he would always come to me saying how he thought we should handle our money: I felt that I had no buy-in. It worked to blame him for a while, but that got boring. I wanted better than blame—I wanted growth, I wanted partnership—so I decided to create my own buy-in by educating myself. I realized that one reason I was so resistant to having money conversations with him was because I felt he was trying to control the structure and the narrative. I felt *powered over*. Although he had good intentions, it came across as his way or no way.

When I discovered a financial structure that had been devised by a money expert, we started making progress together. My husband is an absolute whiz when it comes to numbers, but I am an absolute whiz when it comes to consistent, focused action, and this combination really works for us. We have learned to focus on our strengths, and this has created a successful money partnership. We are both invested in providing for ourselves, our family, and the individuals and communities we support.

Money means freedom to me—freedom to choose, freedom to give, freedom to live.

When I became more financially literate, I was also able to talk to my husband about the importance of having my own bank account that was separate from my business account. Moving on from that, we now have separate bank accounts as well as our family account. I realized I needed to have agency and autonomy with money, which I would not have been able to communicate to him in the past.

As my husband and I are now in established careers, our incomes and assets have grown, and together we have had to understand another level of money management. There is no way that we would be where we are now in our money partnership if I had not decided to become responsible for the gaps in my understanding and be vulnerable enough to ask for support and take responsibility for my own learning. We all have complex and conflicting relationships with money, and knowing this is a source of power in and of itself. As women, we need to be responsible for our money. Many women in heterosexual relationships don't confront their relationship with "men and money" unless the relationship ends. It doesn't matter whether you are in a partnership or a single woman navigating money, we have to confront the gaps in our knowledge and set ourselves up as best we can for our future. You may experience embarrassment if you have gaps in your money knowledge. I still have gaps in my knowledge; I'm learning all the time. But moving from embarrassed to empowered is worth it in the long run.

I promise you, knowing your money is power.

Power Process 23

1. What did you learn about money growing up?
2. Do you feel empowered around the topic of money?
3. Do you need to ask for support from a money professional?

Action: What one action can you take today to enhance your relationship with money?

IV.

THE POWER OF LEADERSHIP

"I define a leader as anyone who takes responsibility for finding the potential in people and processes, and who has the courage to develop that potential."

—Brené Brown

When the book *Dare to Lead* was published, I was about to lead a group of Australian business owners on a leadership immersion program for The Hunger Project in Uganda. I would read to participants from the book nearly every day, and it facilitated open conversations that challenged and confronted every single one of us in some way. We explored unconscious bias, unconscious and conscious racism, gender privilege, and navigating group dynamics.

If I had not been able to address these issues, the potential of the leadership immersion program would have been undermined, and so would the potential of the individual leaders within the group.

As a coach and facilitator, I believe it is my role and responsibility to create a psychologically safe space to have difficult conversations. I believe that exposing the "elephant in the room" is powerful—to name it, to understand the power it has, and then to intentionally set it free before it causes more damage. Elephants are big, and they need all hands on deck to set them free.

"Daring leaders who live into their values are never silent about hard things" is my favorite quote from *Dare to Lead*. This quote was proven by Brené within the first fifteen minutes of the in-person training I attended later that year. Brené walked into the room with a big grin on her face and an even bigger "How are y'all?"

She stood on the stage, looked at us, and asked again, "How are y'all?" And we responded in unison with, "Great! Awesome! Excited!"

Then she said, "This is a very White room."

I love interiors and design, so for a split second I thought she meant the paintwork, and I looked around at the walls—I honestly did.

Then she said, "I know that every single person of color in this room knows exactly how many other people of color there are in this room."

I was at the front of the room and I shouted out, "YES! Five women, one man." I had counted us; I always do.

Then Brené said, "This is something we as an organization are very aware of and something we are actively working on." She went on to read the draft of the "Inclusivity, Equity, and Diversity Statement" that underpins the work of the Brené Brown Education and Research Group.

When she asked for comments, a woman of color in the navy began talking about what the document meant to her. If you asked me what this woman said, I couldn't tell you; I wasn't listening. I was listening instead to the sensation building up in my body. It started at my feet, rose up in me like a wave, and then sat in my heart for a few breaths. I remember thinking, "If someone asked me to speak right now, I couldn't do it. I have no words." I was overcome. Speechless in a way I had never been before.

I am not sure when the wave of sensation made it past my heart, but I do remember huge tears running down my face and thinking, "What is happening?" And then it came to me. "I feel seen. I am seen."

I had never felt seen like that in a White majority in my entire life.

I eventually came back to the room and noticed that one of the other women of color was speaking: five of the seven of us spoke, and the input was consistent through the training.

The next day another woman spoke, and her opening words were, "As a gay woman . . ."

This also continued through the training. The "minority" in the room felt safe enough to be seen because the leader before us had dared to take responsibility and not be silent about hard things, and that brought inclusivity, equity, and diversity into the room.

We all need to be seen as whole and unique. Pretending we are all the same, that we have had the same experiences, diminishes the lived experiences of so many.

From personal experience and in speaking to the other people who identified as a minority in the training, I know that Brené's daring leadership gave us the safety to speak. In taking responsibility for "the elephant in the room," not only did she acknowledge who was not in the room, she allowed those of us in the room to have a voice.

Unless leaders create safety for everyone, they miss out on the types of human connection that allow us all to live and work together in a way that fulfills everyone's potential and maximizes the collective gain as a result.

The world has never needed female leaders the way it needs us now. It has never needed diverse leadership in the way it does now.

If you want to lead, lead.

The world needs you to show up and lead.

Power Process 24

1. If you believed in your leadership capability, what would you do with it?
2. When did you last take responsibility and dare to point out the elephant in the room?
3. How do you want to show up and lead?

Action: What one action can you take today to become a more inclusive leader?

V.

THE POWER OF PRIVILEGE

> *"If you have an advantage, you don't hoard it. You share it. You reach out. You give back."*
>
> **—Michelle Obama**

Privilege is having an advantage that is out of our control, an advantage we didn't ask for, that gives us opportunities. Those without the same privilege as us have to fight harder for these opportunities—or will never have them, no matter how hard they try.

Our race can be our privilege.

Our class can be our privilege.

Our name can be our privilege.

Where we were born can be our privilege.

Being responsible for our privilege is powerful, if we own it and use it responsibly.

Feeling guilty about our privilege has no power at all. To be honest, as far as I am concerned, feeling guilty about privilege is boring.

After years of facilitating groups, I have worked with people from all walks of life, from newly arrived refugees to executives from top companies. I have run retreats with successful women in the corporate or entrepreneurial worlds who feel so guilty about their financial privilege that they don't do anything with it; they are ashamed of their privilege and feel burdened by it. I have facilitated workshops for refugees and migrants who have little financial wealth when they arrive in Australia, but their newfound home "location privilege" has ignited a sense of responsibility toward those who have less than them.

And I have worked with people who sit in all the gray areas in between.

There is always going to be someone who has more privilege than you, and there is always going to be someone with less.

This is what my privilege looks like:

Birthplace privilege: I was born in England.

Language privilege: English is my first language.

Passport privilege: I have a British and an Australian passport.

Socioeconomic privilege: I can buy whatever I need or want.

Location privilege: I live in a major Australian city.

Able-bodied privilege: I do not have a disability.

Cisgendered privilege: I look like and identify as a woman (though I am mistaken for a man at least six times a year!).

Privileges I do not have:

Race privilege.

Gender privilege.

Higher education privilege.

I have no guilt about any of my privilege for two main reasons. One, I do not have race privilege and although this is "softened" in some respects because of my other privileges, it is still the most defining factor of how I am "allowed" to be in the world, followed by my gender.

Secondly, I use my privilege to make a difference. To make a statement. To have an impact. A Black woman once said to me, "We are Black women. By birth we are a political statement."

I am grateful that I am now able to find myself in the places my work and life have taken me. In some of those places, just being there is a mark of my privilege. I own it and I use it.

"Weaponize your privilege" is a phrase that resonates with me deeply. I first saw it spray-painted on a wall and it stopped me in my tracks because it demands action.

We all can use our individual privilege. We can weaponize it and use it as a tool to dismantle the systems that benefit some of us but not all of us.

If you have privilege, don't be ashamed of it. Use it.

Power Process 25

1. What privileges do you have?
2. What privileges do you not have?
3. How can you use your privilege for good?

Action: What one action can you take today to take full responsibility for your privilege?

VI.

THE POWER OF ACTION

There is no doubt that action is scary. There is also no doubt that action is powerful.

As a coach who has worked with hundreds of women in my private practice, I know that action is one of the main reasons my clients want a coach in the first place. People struggle with action. We don't struggle with thinking about taking action, we don't struggle with telling others we are going to take action, we don't struggle in telling others what action they "should" take, but we struggle with taking action ourselves.

Why? Action is exposing. When we take action, we let others see what we are trying to accomplish, and expose what matters most to us.

What if I don't succeed? What if my father was right? What if Mrs. Wilson from primary school was right? What if I fail? What if my action makes the whole team fail? What if my action brings about the end of a relationship? What if my action makes me unlovable?

What if my action brings success?

Life is an unpredictable adventure. There are some parts of it you can control, but in my experience, life is a lesson in letting go of what you can't control and mastering what you can.

Our fear of action is usually grounded in a version of reality: that at some stage you took an action and committed to something that really mattered to you—a person, a job, a competition, the paint color of your bedroom—and it didn't work out. You may have felt embarrassed, humiliated, or ashamed. You may have been embarrassed, humiliated, or shamed by someone else. These feelings overshadow the transformative feelings of courage, bravery, and faith, all of which are needed for meaningful action.

One of my favorite questions to ask as a coach is, What is the impact if you don't take action in this situation? It is a question that delivers again and again in supporting a client to take meaningful action. When we are faced with the consequences of not taking action, action seems like the best move in the end.

When I talk about action, I don't mean action for action's sake: I mean action that is born out of who you want to be and what you want to achieve in the world. I call it meaningful action—actions that have meaning for you.

Action for the sake of action (busy) is not powerful. Being busy is not being in charge of your life; being busy is a way of taking meaningful charge out of life.

"Busy" is a socially accepted form of numbing. Being busy can cover up so much. If we are busy, we can hide our anxiety, our fear, and our disconnection to ourselves and to others. When we are present and in our power, we take meaningful action.

The world does not need busy women, it needs present and powerful women.

When we take action there is a very real chance that it may not work, that the action we take does not give us the result we desired. We may fail.

I know it's not the done thing in some personal development circles to mention the word, but I believe in failure. I think it's good to fall flat on our face sometimes. And when we fail, we so want to jump to the "lesson to be learned," which can be a strategic way of bypassing difficult feelings. Failure is disappointing, frustrating, and sometimes soul-destroying—a heartbreaking failure that causes you to question everything, including yourself.

We may struggle to sit with failure, but that doesn't mean we shouldn't sit with it.

Not everything has a silver lining. Sometimes life just hurts.

We fail. So what? It hurts and we heal (if we are willing to do the work) and then when we are ready, when we have licked our wounds, we move on.

Taking meaningful action in the areas of your life that are important to you does leave you open to failure. It just does. But not taking action in the areas of your life that are important to you leaves you open to a life unlived.

Living a watered-down version of who we want to be in the world or how we want to contribute is never a path to power.

Taking meaningful action that aligns with who you are and what you value gives you access to living with responsibility.

In 2011, when Oprah visited Australia and came to Melbourne, I was there. Of course I was there. She said many powerful words that night, but these words gave me a full-body reaction: "I do nothing by accident. I live with intent."

I remember thinking, "Wow! I want to live with intent, to know what I am doing and why I am doing it."

Every action we take costs something—time, resources, life energy—and every action we don't take also costs us time, resources, and life energy. An important aspect of life is figuring out what costs we are willing to pay, and for what.

Are you open to experiencing failure if it means you can live and lead without apology?

When we take full responsibility for our lives and take meaningful action, we are in our power.

Power Process 26

1. What actions do you need to take to be fully responsible for your life?
2. What actions are you avoiding, and why?
3. What would be a bold action to move toward living with intent?

Action: What one action can you take today to live with more intention?

In summary

Responsibility is my favorite personal and professional development tool. When we take responsibility for what is happening in our lives, we have the power to change it—to create and build something new.

When life is not going the way we want it to, we get to take responsibility for all the actions we did or did not take that got us to where we are now.

Most of us have experienced trauma or multiple traumas in our lives, and if that trauma was perpetrated by another person or persons, the wounding can be debilitating. And yet when we are ready, we can choose to be responsible for our wounding and our healing, because the perpetrators are rarely going to take on that responsibility. Taking responsibility for our healing is difficult and challenging work, so we must find the appropriate support if we want to reclaim what was taken from us—our power.

Values give us a powerful compass to guide meaningful action throughout our lives.

Having responsibility over our money gives us power. It is not all about the amount in the bank: it's how we take responsibility for the money we do have.

Being responsible for our privilege grants us the responsibility and power to effect change when and where we can.

As leaders we need to be responsible for leading ourselves before we can effectively lead others. We have to be responsible for the elephants in the room, so that everyone in that room has the opportunity to step into their full potential.

We have one shot at this gift called life, and we need to take responsibility for directing it, shaping it, and healing through it.

There is power in responsibility.

Part 7

BUILDING POWER

"Fight for the things that you care about, but do it in a way that will lead others to join you."

Ruth Bader Ginsburg

I.

BUILDING POWER

It's time to experience the Power Principles in their full glory.

By the time you have reached this stage in the book, you will have been exposed to twenty-six Power Processes—Power Processes that will have shifted you in big and small ways, perhaps giving you an insight into something you never knew before, an affirmation about a particular situation, or validation for a lived experience.

You may have already taken action from completing these processes. You may have already stepped bravely into a difficult conversation, put a much-needed boundary in place, or let go of a story or imprint that makes you feel powerless.

You are now ready to take your insights, your new awareness, and your actions to build your power base into your future.

We will now move into active application of these insights, through Power Practices. Power Practices are supercharged coaching processes to ignite your reflection, invigorate your action, and awaken you to yourself and your power.

In this final part of the book, we explore the galvanizing forces of practice, community, progress, and vision. The power of practice (not perfection) must never be underestimated, the power of the community that we surround ourselves with must never be ignored, and acknowledging our progress along the way is critical.

Finally, there is our vision. Because, ultimately, what is the point of having power if we don't have a vision big enough to ignite it in the first place?

II.

THE POWER OF PRACTICE

Practice (noun): The actual application or use of an idea, belief, or method, as opposed to theories relating to it.

Throughout this book I mention practicing, because in my experience there is nothing important in our lives that doesn't take practice. For example, love is a practice: the love of oneself and the loving of others. Becoming confident in any skill or task takes practice, and power is no different.

When navigating internal and external forces that make us question our power, we find ourselves feeling powerless more often than we would like. It is challenging to live and lead in a world that favors our smallness. We sometimes step out of our power because we have forgotten who we are, and sometimes our power will be taken away from us. Power is a practice: we have to keep practicing the act of stepping back into our power.

We do not yet live in the world that most of us want to live in. Not yet. I cannot imagine a world where I will not have racist remarks shouted at me from moving cars. I am wise enough to know that I will walk into many more places where I am made to feel that I don't belong because I am Black, and sometimes I will feel my power leave every cell of my body, and I will stand there powerless, watching it leave.

But when I practice building my power, I no longer hustle to "belong" in those places. Not because I have "given up," but because these days I have built my power and I choose where I want to belong. Practicing our power needs to be a lifelong pursuit and building our power is a lifelong investment—not only for us, but for the women who are coming up behind us.

The younger women of today, they are watching us. They are watching us step in and out of our power all the time, in the same way that we watch them stepping in and out of theirs. Is there a better way to give them permission to practice, to fail, and to grow than to generously fail and grow alongside them? To remind them that their power is theirs to own, in the same way that our power is ours to own? Though to be honest, the young women I have the honor of spending time with do not take the shit that my generation was exposed to; we have a lot to learn from them.

Do you know who else is watching you? Your future self. Your future self is created in the practices you choose today, tomorrow, and beyond.

So we can ask ourselves, "What would I guide a younger woman to do in this situation?" or we can ask, "What would my future self want me to do in this situation?"

Some days we will feel stronger than others, and that is fine. This is when we get present to what is going on, take ownership where we can, tap into our wisdom, step into equality, and take full responsibility.

A great way to practice your power is to take one of the Power Stories in this book and the Power Process attached to it and work with it for a while. Or take to your journal and unravel your imprints.

Building our power is an ongoing commitment to owning ourselves and our space in the world, and an ongoing commitment to supporting other women to do the same.

Practice owning your thoughts, your words, your voice, your power.

As you continue to question what you have been told, learned, and experienced about power in the past, there may be an internal reckoning. This can take various forms, including self-blame, regret, anger, and grief, to name a few. And this is when the ultimate Power Practices come into play: the practices of self-compassion, forgiveness, and self-care.

Looking after yourself takes practice; looking after yourself builds power.

III.

ACKNOWLEDGING PROGRESS

When working with clients, I encourage them to measure their progress. I do this because the brain has a negativity bias—it will always look for what is missing—so we have to practice acknowledging what has been gained and learned along the way.

A misconception I often find is that people think progress has to be a big leap or life-changing. But that is not my lived experience or the experience of my clients.

Let's take the example of the story I shared in "Equality" of my conversation with the client who was not respecting our contract, which led to me owning my worth. In the past I would have assumed that he was in the right, by default. That I as a Black woman who should be "grateful" should not speak truth to the power of the White male and should not cause a fuss.

Progress for me in that situation was to no longer assume he was right and I was wrong. Progress was me knowing that I was worthy of professional respect, regardless of the power dynamic at play. The awareness was my progress.

I have worked with clients who feel they are not making progress because the world did not shift on its axis straight away. But they miss that they have shifted their internal axis in various ways. For example, when we stop accepting the status quo as truth, we make progress. When we go in for the difficult conversation that we would never have attempted before, we make progress, regardless of the outcome. When we speak up and our heart is pounding, we make progress.

Not all progress is earth-shattering. In fact, it is more likely to be the smaller moments compounding on each other that will give you bigger and more sustainable rewards. Progress can be measured with meaningful goal setting. It can be measured through reflective practices such as journaling, and it can also be measured through feeling. How do you feel walking into that room now? How do you feel having that difficult conversation? Setting boundaries may have felt difficult, but if you never would have put a boundary in place before, it's progress.

There is no one way to measure progress, because it looks and feels different for everybody. What is crucial is that you acknowledge your progress. If giving yourself a pat on the back and acknowledging is a difficult practice for you, find a person or community who will acknowledge you and your progress while you are learning to do it for yourself.

Progress is power.

IV.

THE POWER OF COMMUNITY

Community (noun): A group of people living in the same place or having a particular characteristic in common.

Community gives us a sense of belonging to a collective of people who are coming together to build something bigger than each individual, though each individual brings their own unique gifts and enthusiasm. The gift of a powerfully created community means that we do not have to journey alone.

The *Oxford English Dictionary* says a community is "a group of people living in the same place," which can be true, but I have lived in places where there has been no sense of community at all. Proximity does not a community make. It takes effort and vulnerability to build community, to stand side by side and be a powerful resource for each other.

As women, we are diverse. We have different ethnicities, cultural backgrounds, ages, life stages, and economic situations, and yet the fact that we navigate the world as women can be enough to create community. We don't have to agree on all issues; we don't have to want the same things—we don't even need to like each other—but it is about having a respect for our shared experience of gender.

As we change and grow through life, the support of the communities we need changes and grows as well. I have a few different communities of women that I belong to, some based on friendship, some that are interest based, some based on shared ethnicity and culture, some that are work based, and some that tick all the boxes. All of these communities of women empower and support me in many different ways, and I would not want to navigate life without them.

The communities of women I have attracted or created have met me where I was, at that time. When I was a gossip, I was surrounded with gossips; when I was partying, I was surrounded by people who liked to party; and when I became a parent, it was the same. Some communities we find ourselves in are built by default and some are meticulously curated. I have both in my life.

And I have expectations of the communities I am a part of. When I am with a group of women, I need to feel more of who I am, not less. I need to feel that I can contribute my unique gifts and not feel judged for them. I need to walk away with more energy, not less. I need to feel a sense of connection and a shared respect for the time we have spent together. I need to know that as a collective we are supporting each other to thrive, whatever that means for each individual woman.

What are some of the factors that create your communities of women? Think about the women you share your life with. Are you getting what you need from them? Do they accept what you bring to the table? Are you able to share who you are, what matters to you, and what you are creating for your future?

If not, build the community that you can serve and nourish and that will serve and nourish you in return. It doesn't mean cutting people out of your life (although sometimes it does). What it *does* mean is committing to being in spaces where you can be fully seen for who you are without guilt or apology.

Life can be incredibly hard. We are social beings, and we need the support of others to truly thrive. We were not meant to do life alone.

As women, we can lean on each other, wipe away each other's blood, sweat, and tears, and help each other back up when life throws us a devastating curveball.

As women, we have the opportunity to embolden, enliven, and empower each other to stand up, use our voices, and be seen.

As women, we get to choose the communities we create and the communities we belong to. I invite you to choose wisely.

We can create new futures for each other, together.

V.

POWER PRACTICES

Now it is your turn to bring everything you have read and discovered about yourself into full focus. To cement your insights and learnings, here are a variety of practices to support you to build and maintain your power.

There are five Power Practices:

1. Power Practice List

2. Power Questions

3. The Power of "I Am . . ."

4. The Power of Ten Decisions

5. Power Project

You may want to take yourself through all of these practices, or you may decide to choose one and see where it leads you. What is important is that you take it easy. One shift. One action. At a time.

VI.

POWER PRACTICE LIST

Having a Power Practice List is useful for when you feel disempowered—your list can be your reference point. You can use it to check in on why you feel disempowered and if there is something you need to take responsibility for.

Ask yourself these questions: *How am I present? How am I taking ownership? How am I owning my wisdom? How am I stepping into equality? How am I taking responsibility?*

The ability to check in on where you have lost your power is the foundation for knowing how to build it back up again.

What you choose to put on your list is going to be a mix of who you are, what is important to you, and who is important to you. There is no perfect list or correct list; there is only the one that works for you. As you become more and more practiced at building and maintaining your power, your list will change and grow as you do.

Let me share my Power Practice List with you. Here are ten ways I build and maintain my power:

1. I spend time each morning being present to my thoughts, feelings, and energy levels with a mix of meditation, journaling, and physical movement.

2. I have very clear boundaries that have been put in place to honor who I am and what and who is important to me. If I feel overwhelmed, I know it's a boundary issue, it's not about the other person.

3. I spend time in nature every day, even if it's only for ten minutes. It connects me to myself and reminds me that I am part of something much bigger.

4. I spend a lot of time resting and doing not much at all; it builds my reserves and expands my creativity. And when I'm on vacation, I'm one hundred percent on vacation.

5. I am at a stage in my career where I get to choose the people and organizations I work with, something I don't take for granted.

6. I am always aiming to peel back my own layers with the help of professional coaches and mentors, to understand my own inner workings—the good, the bad, and the ugly.

7. I do my best in everything I do. If I'm not willing to do my best, it's not something I'm interested in doing.

8. I am very discerning about what gets my attention, and I make no apology for what I choose.

9. I am not a consumer of media that disempowers me or its subjects, or focuses on inducing fear.

10. I have a small inner circle where I can show all parts of me without fear or apology.

And my galvanizing Power Practice is that once a year I spend a full week completely alone at home fasting, doing yoga every day, sleeping a lot, and spending time reflecting, walking, writing, and creating the year ahead.

All these practices and learnings were developed over the

past twenty years, and I know they will change and grow as I change and grow.

As mentioned before, we will continually step into and out of our power. I want to keep reminding you that this is not a linear process. You will take steps forward and steps backward—it is all part of the process.

We can feel power in how we walk down the street, and then we turn a corner or a stranger looks at us in a certain way, and our power of presence has gone.

We start a business and we feel that it is not what we wanted to create, that others are messing it up for us, and our power of ownership has gone.

We step into our power with a work project, and we return home and our toddler screams, "No! No! No!" to dinner; we give them what they want instead, and our power of wisdom is gone.

We can feel the power of equality in our intimate relationship, and then our dad calls, and our power of equality has gone.

We may find ourselves living a life that does not fulfill us, where we don't feel we are contributing, and all we do is complain about it, and our power of responsibility has gone.

Sometimes events happen that take our power away. But if we have a foundation of practice, it will return. Your Power Practice List will guide you.

POWER is a practice.

VII.

THE POWER OF "I AM . . ."

When I have finished working with a client, one of the coaching processes I may guide them through is the process called "I am . . ."

Within personal and professional development work, we often hear the same messages from different people, the reason being that they are powerful messages. I first came across the concept of "I am . . ." when I heard Joel Osteen being interviewed for his book *The Power of I Am*. It was then that I decided to curate my own version of it for my clients. Five years later in the Dare to Lead™ training, Brené Brown also used the concept of "I am . . ." I want to share with you two ways of using "I am . . ." to build your power.

In one method, I ask my clients to tell me who they are and who they have stepped into being during our work together by sharing three phrases that start with "I am . . ."

Responses I have heard include:

I am brave.

I am learning.

I am enough.

I am worthy.

I am kind.

I am ambitious.

In "Ownership," Jeanette-Margaret shared in her Power Story the poem she wrote about speaking her birth name. This took place during a Dare to Lead™ retreat where I had facilitated a process that included writing a poem called "I am . . ." This is another coaching process I use with my clients.

I want to share with you my current version of this poem:

I am Kemi. I am of Nigerian heritage and an English and Australian citizen. I am Black. I am of fostered stock. I am a multi-passionate and I am proud of this fact. I am here to serve. I am a lover of boundaries. I am an introvert. I am a lover of beauty in its many forms. I am wounded. I am a creator. I am a connector. I am a maker and a grower. I am in my body. I am someone who feels things strongly. I am a true and loyal friend. I am a good enough mother and a "top-shelf" wife. I am flawed. I am not an apology. I am growing. I am whole. I am worthy.

And now it is your turn.

Who are you? What has made you who you are? What has brought you to this exact moment in your life?

Begin by writing the words "I am . . . ," and keep going.

VIII.

THE POWER OF TEN DECISIONS

When listening to *The Tim Ferriss Show* recently, I heard one of his guests talking about the ten biggest decisions they had ever made in their life. It got me thinking about the ten biggest decisions I have made in my life. All of them were courageous, most of them hard. Let me share them with you:

1. Leaving my first true love and choosing to be celibate for two and a half years.

2. Leaving a well-paid acting career to work for free in Thailand.

3. Deciding to have a baby with a man I'd known for nine months.

4. Moving to Australia while six months pregnant with said baby to live with my in-laws, whom I'd only met once.

5. Choosing to have a second baby and get married.

6. Writing my first book.

7. Training for and finishing my first marathon.

8. Training as a credentialed coach (always in training).

9. Training as a Dare to Lead™ facilitator (always in training).

10. Buying our farm and acreage.

All my biggest decisions involved Presence, Ownership, Wisdom, Equality, and Responsibility.

I needed to be present to how I was feeling in a particular situation; I needed to take ownership for my stories and let go of the stories of others; I needed to listen to my own wisdom, even when it made no sense to other people; I needed to see myself as an equal to make the life choices I wanted to make; and I needed to take responsibility for the implementation and outcomes of all of these decisions.

So often, we forget the times we have been courageous, when we have stood in our power, claimed our space, owned our worth, and gone after what we needed or wanted. It does not mean these decisions are easy. In fact, big decisions are rarely easy—that's the point of your ten biggest decisions.

Take a moment now to think about the ten biggest decisions you have made in your life so far. Even better, write them down and then answer these questions:

1. Which decision are you proudest of?

2. What does your list tell you about who you are?

3. What does your list tell you about your power?

The power of the decisions we have made in the past is an evidence-based way to build our power into the future.

One of the greatest tools my coach Belinda gave me was the power of evidence. If I was questioning my ability in something she would say, "Let's find the evidence that questions your doubt." It is such a powerful tool, and when appropriate, it's a tool I now use with my clients.

Your list of your ten biggest decisions is your evidence—proof that you have stood in your power before, no matter how hard, lonely, terrifying, or confusing it may have been. You have been powerful before and your power has guided you through life.

You can be powerful now and you can be powerful in the future.

IX.

THE POWER QUESTIONS

Welcome to the Power Questions: a set of prompts to help you go deeper into the areas of your life where you want to build your power. These questions are a big-picture examination of power in your life, a chance to look at the Power Principles and think about how each area of your life is affected by them—and based on this, to project into the future. They are:

1. In what area of my life do I need to be more present?

2. In what area of my life do I need to take ownership?

3. In what area of my life do I need to trust my wisdom?

4. In what area of my life do I need to create equality for myself and for others?

5. In what area of my life do I need to take full responsibility?

6. In which situations do I question my power?

7. What person or group of people negatively impacts my power?

8. If I fully honored my power I could . . .

Once you have answered these questions, you are ready to create your Power Project.

X.

YOUR POWER PROJECT

By the time you get to this part of the book, you will know the areas of your life in which you feel powerless. They will have popped up in your answers when you were doing the Power Processes in each chapter, and your awareness of your lack of power in these situations would have revealed itself not only as you read the book, but also as you went about your life.

It is now time to shift your power, one action at a time.

First, choose *one* area of your life in which you want to build your power: work, intimate relationship, family, money . . . There may be more than one, but let's start with one and you can build from there.

Then, answer the following questions to measure the power you feel in this area of life, the traits you need to practice, and the actions you need to take:

1. On a scale of 1 to 10 (10 being the highest—but don't use 7, as it's the number we use to stay safe) how much power do you feel you currently have in this area?

2. Which of the five Power Principles do you need to practice in this area? Presence, Ownership, Wisdom, Equality, Responsibility?

3. What would success look like in this area of your life?

4. What empowered feelings would be present in this area of your life?

5. How will you know you are making progress?

6. What are the first three actions you need to take to build your power base in this area of your life?

Working with our power is not easy work. It requires addressing unconscious imprints and beliefs that can be quite challenging, and generally involves difficult and vulnerable conversations—which is why I suggest having one Power Project at a time. Be kind to yourself by focusing on one area and seeing what reveals itself to you. Also, as you work on one area, there will be shifts and changes in other areas too.

One of the most important things here is to not overwhelm yourself: overwhelm is not powerful. This is your Power Project. It is not meant to overwhelm you, it has been created to empower you. One compassionate action at a time.

XI.

THE POWER OF VISION

As I conclude this book, I am left with a feeling of what is possible for women. As individuals, we must have an awareness of where our power truly lies—then we will be able to act in a particular way.

When we are fully aware of the times we give our power away and we understand why, we can move back into power. In those moments when your power is diminished, ask yourself the question: *What would power do now?* You will know. An answer will come to you and then you will get to act in a particular way.

My intention in writing this book is for you—for me, for us—to be comfortable with power. You may want to create a mantra for yourself: "I have power" or "I am power." If you're thinking that saying these phrases is a waste of time, you need to understand the power of mantras. We need to keep telling ourselves a different story, repeating it so that we can begin to believe it. *We* need to shift the power paradigm: no one else is going to do it for us.

And if you find yourself in a place where your power feels lost, know you have the tools to examine why, what the moment was when you gave it away, and what you will do to claim it back.

Power is innate in all of us. It looks different, it feels different, but it is innate.

Your voice has power.

Your skills have power.

Your wounds have power.

Your story has power.

Your dreams have power.

Your success has power.

You have power.

As I said at the very start of this book, power is the ability to do something in a certain way. What do you want to do with your power? What is your vision?

Let me share my vision with you.

My vision is to use my voice and my skill set to ignite power in women.

My vision is for every woman, regardless of race, to feel that she belongs in any tier of society she wants to be in, but more importantly, I want her to know that she belongs to herself first. Not to her parents or her siblings, not to her partner or her children—you, dear woman, belong to yourself.

My vision is that when my children reach my age, they will scoff at the inequities women inherited, lived with, and in some ways perpetuated. They will laugh that there was ever a disparity between the genders or the "worthiness" of one race over another.

My vision is that when I stand onstage to speak, every woman who sees me up there understands that if she too wants to speak, she can, without apology.

My vision is that we use our collective power to shake up the status quo in big and little ways. We need to keep shaking and dismantling. We have come a long, long way, but there is still a long, long way to go.

Think about the power of the suffragettes, the power of the Civil Rights Movement and the disrupters of oppressive regimes such as apartheid: they wanted something done in a particular way, so they led the way. Their power came from the wisdom of knowing that something was inherently wrong with how they or others were being treated, just like the #MeToo and Black Lives Matter movements today. Their power came from a vision of wanting something different and in owning their leadership—people followed, and they all acted in a particular way together. And as their movements gained momentum, as they started to become a thorn in the side of the status quo of the *power over* model, they began to understand the power they had to change things. Because if a power structure, when threatened, puts everything it has into discrediting, oppressing, and stopping you from asserting your power, you're onto something.

Keep going.

My vision is that those of us who live in a level of privilege, who live in a safe country, and who do not have to fear brutal and misogynistic practices such as female genital mutilation and child marriage can use our power to remind our global sisters of theirs. Not step in and take their power away from them, but remind them of theirs—there is a difference.

Through my work with The Hunger Project, I was told the story of Rumi. She is one of 30,000 girls who have been trained in The Hunger Project's Safe Schools for Girls program.

Rumi was fourteen years old and living in Bangladesh with her parents, who were among the poorest in the village. Over time, her father was unable to keep up with her school fees.

Rumi was taken out of school and her parents started arranging her marriage.

Rumi spoke in a video on The Hunger Project's website about

her story: "I felt like my life had stopped. My dreams were shattered when I was taken out of school. I wasn't ready to become a mother or a wife. I was devastated."

Rumi had to stay at home while her marriage was being arranged, and one of her close friends was missing her at school and went to visit Rumi to find out what was wrong. Rumi told her friend that her parents were forcing her to marry.

The next day her friend asked their mutual classmates, "What shall we do now?"

All arrangements for the marriage had been set, and suddenly Rumi's classmates, a group of fourteen-year-old girls, arrived at Rumi's home and said to her father, "She has her whole life ahead of her. It is not right to marry her off as a child!"

"My father began to see that child marriage is not right, that it could destroy my life," said Rumi.

The friends were not finished. Next, they went to see the headmistress and said that if the school could pay the cost of Rumi's education, her parents would not need to force her to get married so young. Some of the teachers went to Rumi's house and told her parents that they would start a school fund for the poorer families so students like Rumi could receive a free education. Rumi went back to school, is studying hard, and has a dream of becoming a doctor.

These fourteen-year-old leaders had the power and the courage to act in a particular way and they used it. Never underestimate the power of fourteen-year-old girls to change their world.

And never again underestimate the power you have to change yours.

XII.

FULL CIRCLE

I was sitting at the dinner table with my fourteen-year-old after they had a hard day at school. At the time they were one of a handful of children of color in a school of 1,500 students. They were conscious of and were made conscious of being a minority every day.

We were talking about race and belonging, and I asked, "Are you comfortable in your own skin, darling?"

Ibi looked me straight in the eye and said, "Are you kidding?! You're my mother! I am so proud to be Black!"

I could not hold back my tears. At fourteen, I had tried to end my life because I had no power in what was happening to me; I did not feel that I belonged in any place. It has been a difficult and painful road to get to here in a world that has repeatedly told me I was powerless. But I wouldn't change any of it, because I have learned how to build my power from the inside out and it has allowed my child to be proud of who they are.

A full circle moment.

And now, as a fifteen-year-old, they have become Ibiyemi (their Nigerian name)—Ibi for short—and use the pronouns "they/them." They are living and leading without apology.

Every day we are writing our stories. We write them with our words, our thoughts, our actions, and our being.

I invite you to own your story and your power. Let's all live and lead together, without apology.

ACKNOWLEDGMENTS

To my dear friend Michelle Conder, thank you for planting the seed of this book and walking alongside me in so many ways.

To my friend and mentor Andrew Griffiths, thank you for being there in "that moment" when the title came, and for opening up new worlds for me.

To my inner circle, I adore how we support each other in life and in business, living and leading without apology and picking each other up when (not if) we fall. Your loyalty is everything.

To all of the women in this book who have generously shared their stories of power, this book would not be what it is without your contributions. I am deeply grateful.

To my clients who courageously take on what is and is not working in their lives, so that they can live and lead without apology. You inspire me daily and it is a privilege to work with you.

To Julia Luyten, thank you for taking care of everything behind the scenes with your steady hand.

To my agent Pippa, thank you for your "presence" and the one-word debriefs!

To the Penguin Random House team:

To Izzy, thank you for taking a chance and loving this book before I even knew what it was going to be. You appeared at just the right time. Your partnership is the stuff of publishing dreams.

To my stellar editing team:

Rachel Scully—thank you for your guidance, your questions, your grounded skill, and your open heart. Our conversations made all the difference. It has been an absolute gift to work with you.

Kalhari Jayaweera—thank you. I don't even know how you do what you do, but thank you for doing it with humor and a lived "knowing" of some of my experiences. Your abundant skills have elevated this book.

You are both a blessing.

To my family, Emrys, Benjamin, and Ibiyemi. Thank you for your subtle and overt ways of supporting me as I wrote this book, especially leaving me alone to write this book!

We have reached a new chapter as a family; watching you all live and lead without apology empowers and inspires me daily. I love you.

To you, the reader, with so many things competing for your attention, I thank you for choosing to read my words.

STAYING CONNECTED

Say hello:
Website: www.keminekvapil.com
Instagram: @Keminekvapil
LinkedIn: Keminekvapil

Gifts:
Download your free *POWER* resources and free Self-Coaching Check-In at www.keminekvapil.com.

Words:
Subscribe to my *Weekly Words* newsletter via my website to receive weekly insights and musings on leadership and life, and upcoming events.

Podcast:
Listen in to *The Shift Series*—a short-form podcast comprising a collection of coaching prods that allow you to tap into your inner resources, create meaningful actions, and shift forward in your life.